Endorsements

I have known Dorinda Trick for over ten years and can say she has an understanding of the triune nature of human beings like few others. Dorinda has spoken to my spirit through this ground-breaking book, and I pray this book will speak to your spirit as well. I highly recommend *Opening the Gift!*

— *Dr. Charles Robinson, CEO*
WISE Ministries International
author of "Let Heaven Invade the Seven Mountains of Culture" series
speaker and spiritual, life, and executive coach

Understanding the why and the what for your presence on this planet are two of the most important issues every human has to face. Unknown potential will be unleashed after reading *Opening the Gift*, because you will begin to understand your true identity in Christ. Dorinda has definitely captured God's heart toward us in this book.

— *Pastor Scott Schatzline, Lead Pastor*
Daystar Family Church

The teaching in this book has helped me in my business and my mission, because understanding my redemptive gift has given me a greater depth of knowledge of myself and the role I play in the world. I believe it has freed me to be more of who I am and what I was meant to be.

— *D. Farah, CEO and founder*
Bajalia International Group

OPENING
the GIFT

Discover

Your True Identity

in God

DORINDA TRICK

SPIRIT-LED
PUBLISHING

Opening the Gift

Copyright © 2015 by Dorinda Trick

Special discounts are available on quantity purchases by corporations, associations, and others. Orders by US trade bookstores and wholesalers—for details, contact the author at the e-mail address above.

Scripture quotations are from THE HOLY BIBLE, NEW INTERNATIONAL VERSION®, NIV® Copyright © 1973, 1978, 1984, 2011 by Biblica, Inc.® Used by permission. All rights reserved worldwide.

All Scripture quotations marked, 'MSG' from THE MESSAGE. Copyright © by Eugene H. Peterson 1993, 1994, 1995, 1996, 2000, 2001, 2002. Used by permission of Tyndale House Publishers, Inc.

Quotations from *Designed for Fulfillment—A Study of the Redemptive Gifts* by Charles Wale Jr. © used by permission from Arsenal Books, www.arsenalbooks.com

Quotations from *Blessing Your Spirit* by Sylvia Gunter and Arthur Burk © 2005 used by permission from Sylvia Gunter, The Father's Business, P. O. Box 380333, Birmingham, AL 35238, www.thefathersbusiness.com

Editor: Inksnatcher
Cover design: Allison Metcalfe Design
Photo of Dorinda Trick: Sabrina Harless Photography
First Edition, 2015
ISBN: 978-1-943011-00-1
Publisher: Spirit-Led Publishing

I dedicate this book to my Father God for His great grace in healing my identity and the identity of countless others who have ached to know their true birthright in God. I also dedicate this to the one who has shared my struggles and loved me unconditionally through it all—my husband, Fred. Fred, you are a beautiful blend of the redemptive gifts of Giver and Ruler ... a person truly sold out to the vision of God. I am grateful for God's grace in bringing me such a strong and steady partner in Christ.

Table of Contents

Introduction

Designed by God

"AS FAR as I can remember, I struggled with identity, purpose, and destiny. Life taught me to build a protective wall around myself and live through my soul, emotions, feelings, people, and things. Everyday life was like going into a battleground unarmed.

"What happens when you go unarmed is that you risk getting attacked, beaten, robbed, and worse (physically, mentally, and spiritually). Deep inside I just knew it couldn't be right to live like this for the rest of my life. God answers prayers! This teaching has been a lifesaver. My spirit has been nurtured, restored, trained, and made strong. My relationship to God has become closer. I have been healed from some things, seen more visions, have more joy, and smile a lot more.

"I am now learning to allow my spirit— that is alive in Christ—to be over my soul, not the other way around. I was hearing Christ but then directing His words through my soul and flesh and dismissing my spirit."

— Client

This is the testimony of a young woman who received what you will (hopefully) receive after reading this book. She received instruction about her design from God—spirit, soul, and body. She learned what her spiritual identity and legitimacy is in Christ. She knows who she is now, who God made her to be.

This is her birthright. It is yours too.

It's sad but true—many people do not have a clear sense of who they are. They feel confused about themselves and their purposes in life. It all boils down to a lack of identity and legitimacy. Beyond knowing and believing in their own identity and legitimacy as human beings, many people simply have no grasp of the purposes of their lives or the reasons they were born. They fail to recognize there is actually an eternal purpose for their lives, one which can only be found when they discover God's design for who they are.

God's unique design for your identity points you directly to your purpose for existing in the first place, not to mention all you are made to do while here on planet earth. When you begin to see you have been designed to fulfill a true and everlasting purpose, it frees you to begin to move out in the things God created you to do. Only this will bring you true fulfillment.

"I have come that they may have life, and have it to the full" (John 10:10b).

෴

You may already be a Christian but know there is something more. You know there is untapped potential inside you. You need to recognize and receive the truth of your identity and purpose in God. You need to discover who it is God made you to be.

—OR—

You may be a seeker, someone who is turned off by "God-talk" but who has struggled (as I did for many years) with making sense of your life. You are ready to have peace of mind about who you are and your purpose in life.

෴

In this book, you will receive answers to questions like:

• Who am I, really? Did God truly make me like this or am I just a big mistake?

- Can I find greater fulfillment in my life, truly feel at peace with God, and know I'm in His will?

- When I find my purpose, will I know how to operate in it?

- Why did God give me personality traits like these?

Even if you don't believe in God, trust Him, or think He gives a whit about who you are and who you are made to be, would you consider suspending your beliefs and allow yourself an opportunity to entertain a new perspective? If you agree to do this, I believe you will see that discovering your true identity and purpose is the way to true life.

Pet that devil ???

Chapter 1

It Begins with a Blessing

"**I HAVE** *not been able to get the information [about this] out of my head. (I guess that is the point though.) I have been speaking to my spirit a lot lately and asking it to instruct my soul. Last night at prayer, I asked my spirit to come to the front and for my soul to move aside so my spirit could communicate without hindrance with the Holy Spirit. I could tell a difference. So I know I am on a journey for life to unpack that which God placed in me even before I entered planet earth.*"

— Special Education Specialist

"LAST NIGHT *after the spiritual nurturing class, I felt like my spirit was soaring high. I blessed each of my children individually. I called my mom and blessed her, and sent my dad and brother a blessing as well. Today I brought the blessing book to work, and after blessing a baby in one class, I stopped someone else and blessed her, and yet another person after that. The last person suggested I do it on a regular basis at the preschool where I work. I thought it was a great idea, so I went and talked to the boss and she approved of me doing a blessing every Tuesday, at a designated time, with whoever wanted to come. My spirit still feels like I am on a high ... a holy ghost high!*"

— T. Bryant

"Help! My life does not make sense."

Can you relate to this statement? If no one was around, would you be willing to admit it was true?

I was forty-seven years old before my life began to make sense, and it all began with a blessing. I don't want to make you wait, so here's the blessing. It is front and center in this book because it is the starting point of your journey toward greater identity and legitimacy in the Lord. Read it aloud to yourself. You will recognize it is quite powerful. It comes from the Word of God. [Note: One meaning for blessing, according to Merriam-Webster's Collegiate Dictionary, is a statement of divine favor. It is a way of asking for God's divine favor to rest upon you and others. The ancient blessing in Numbers reflects five things Aaron and his sons were to ask God for, for the people of Israel: "May the Lord bless you and protect you. May the Lord smile on you and be gracious to you. May the Lord show you his favor and give you his peace" (Numbers 6:24-26 NLT). God told Moses He wanted Aaron and his sons (who were the priests for the people) to "put" God's name upon the people and bless them.]

The Blessing of Identity and Legitimacy

_____, I call your spirit to attention in the name of Jesus of Nazareth. Listen to the Word of God for you.

"For you created my inmost being; you knit me together in my mother's womb. I praise you because I am fearfully and wonderfully made; your works are wonderful, I know that full well. My frame was not hidden from you when I was made in the secret place. When I was woven together in the depths of the earth, your eyes saw my unformed body. All the days ordained for me were written in your book before one of them came to be."

_____, your Father made you special. You are a very special person created, crafted, and designed by God your Father. Before the foundation of the world, your Father planned for you. You are no accident. You did not have to exist, but your Father willed you into existence. He chose the day and the time you would start your life. He chose your parents and wove you together in your mother's womb. He planned your birth order and put you in your family. He chose every one of your twenty-three pairs of chromosomes. He chose every one of your 10,000 plus genes. He chose every part of your spiritual heritage. He reached back into your mother's bloodline, your father's bloodline, and generations past and chose from different parts of your heritage—some not so beautiful, but others absolutely gorgeous. Your Father wove it all together and gave you everything you need (in the package of your life) to be an overcomer and victor—one to take the negative parts of your heritage, triumph over them, and walk in the beauty of all God has placed within you. Your Father made you beautiful and beloved.

I bless you, _____ , because you are fearfully and wonderfully made. God invested an incredible amount of effort in designing you. You are unique and one of a kind. There is nobody else like you. God has thought extensively about you. Every detail of your body, each organ, and each cell is the result of God's thoughts. Every facet of your personality is a result of His kind intention. You are beautiful and you are beloved. God has blessed you with His love. God smiled on the day He created you. He had been waiting for millennia for the particular point in time when you would be conceived. He had great joy in His heart when His plans came together. He nurtures your spirit; He watches over you. Your world needs you. You bring something to your family that no other person has. They need the gifts you bring. Your family would not be complete without you. Others in your circle need the deposit God has placed in your life.

_____ , your Father has written your days in His book. He has already read the final chapters, although we have not had that privilege. Your life is not a random thing. He is looking forward to the chapters of the story He has already written. He designed your spiritual heritage. Your generational blessings go back a thousand generations. There is a spiritual treasure chest of generational blessings with your name on it. Those are being released to you incrementally over the course of your life at the appointed and appropriate times. All this is in God's master plan. God has foreseen your pain. He promises that because of His love, His power, and His blessing upon you, pain and negative things will be transformed into good things before the end of the story of your life. I don't know all the future may hold for you, but I do know you are loved, you are a blessing to your family, and you are a life-giver in this world. You are special, and I celebrate God's miraculous design of who you are. I bless you in the name of Jesus Christ. Amen. (From *Blessing Your Spirit* by Sylvia Gunter and Arthur Burk).

⌒

The blessing you just read comes from Psalm 139: 13-16, a pretty famous passage in the Bible. It is well known to many Christians, but whether you recognize it or not, it's likely you've never been told who you are in this way. You may have also noticed the blessing is directed to your spirit. One thing you will learn in this book is that directing truth to the innermost part of your being—your spirit—makes all the difference in the world.

The first time I received the blessing, I didn't really understand what my spirit was. If you'd asked me if I had one, I'm not sure I could have answered that question. Since accepting Jesus into my life, no one had ever addressed my spirit with me, and somehow it seemed off limits. My thinking on the subject (if I thought about it at all) sounded something like: It's best to wait for someone else to bring this up because of the risk of misunderstanding. So before the blessing I was a believer in Christ, but I was not experiencing the life of strength, freedom, and peace He promises in His Word.

When I received the blessing, tears of relief and a deep sense of gratitude overwhelmed me. I realized I had just experienced the acknowledgement and love of the Lord in the deepest part of my being for the first time in my life!

Before the blessing, I was clueless. I had no language to express, or understanding of, the missing pieces in my life, yet I was more than ready for identity and legitimacy to take hold. No doubt, the blessing brought healing to me. Like a heat-seeking missile that finds its specific target, the words "God willed you into existence'" exploded inside me! The hidden shame and defectiveness I had long been entrenched in simply broke off my life. It was amazing! I'd read Psalm 139 before, but this time, when the words of truth were directed to my spirit, I felt a freedom and peace I had never known before.

The blessing helped me begin to understand my life in a new way. The truth of God's Word was making sense of my life.

Divine Design

What gives? What makes the blessing so powerful? The reason the blessing makes such an impact is because it is directed to your spirit. God designed you to receive your deepest sense of legitimacy (i.e., belonging, competence, worth, His love) in your spirit. Why? Because He wants you to live life led by your spirit.

His Word confirms this: "May God Himself, the God of peace, sanctify you through and through. May your whole spirit, soul and body be kept blameless at the coming of our Lord Jesus Christ. The one who calls you is faithful, and he will do it" (I Thessalonians 5:23-24). The blueprint is clear and specific—your spirit is primary. It was made by God to lead your life.

An Important Distinction—Spirit and Soul

God gives a spirit to every person. "[It is] the Spirit of God that made me [which has stirred me up], and the breath of the Almighty that gives me life [which inspires me]" (Job 33:4 AMP). Your spirit comes from God: "Thus says the Lord, Who

— 9 —

... forms the spirit of man within him" (Zechariah 12:1 AMP) and "Then the Lord God formed man from the dust of the ground and breathed into his nostrils the breath or spirit of life" (Genesis 2:7 AMP).

Your spirit and the Holy Spirit of God mirror one another, both in nature and function. The primary job of the Holy Spirit is to communicate life to your spirit. "The Spirit gives life; the flesh counts for nothing" (John 6:63). Likewise, your own spirit is made by God to be the communicator of life to your soul and your body. (You may have recognized the truth in this statement as you've watched elderly loved ones give up their spirit and die soon afterwards, oftentimes following a loved one—such as a spouse—who has died before them).

Your spirit is the most vital, innermost part of your being. It's your essence, the part of you that does not require your body for expression. Your soul is dependent on your body to express itself. Your spirit is not.

Both your spirit and your soul have thoughts, will, and emotions. This is illustrated in the following example:

A man goes for surgery. He is put under general anesthesia. The anesthesia shuts down his body and soul (because without a body through which the soul can express itself, the soul is shut down). At this point he is no longer able to express his feelings about the experience he is having. He may feel frustrated by all the hospital red tape, or aggravated by the disorganization of the nursing staff, or wishing he could tell someone to please bump up the thermostat in the operating room. (It's cold!) These are the thoughts, feelings, and will of the soul.

But the spirit is free of the restrictions placed on the soul by a body under anesthesia. Many people share the experience of leaving their bodies during surgery and going to an upper corner of the operating room, where they look down on the scene below them. Sometimes they speak of entering a long tunnel of light, at the end of which is a place with grass so green, colors so vibrant, and a sense of peace and joy such as they've never known before that it seems like heaven. There they meet Jesus or a loved one, with whom they argue to try and stay, but they're told it's not their time yet; they still have work to do. They then return through the tunnel, reenter the operating room, and watch the team furiously working to bring them back to life, at which point their spirit reenters the body and life returns to it.

As you can see in this example (a story which we seem to be hearing more and more these days), the spirit of the person is not affected by the anesthesia at all, and the spirit clearly has a mind, will, and emotions of its own. We know this because of the thoughts, feelings, and desires that are reported later.

You may be thinking, *Well that's nice that your spirit shows up when you are about to die, but what about the rest of the time? Where is my spirit?*

The Status of Man's Spirit Today: DOA
(Dormant on Arrival)

In the beginning, God breathed His life into man, making him spiritually alive. Sin later separated Adam and Eve from God and spiritual death occurred. As a result, you are born with a spirit that is dead toward God.

Disconnected from God for many years, my soul searched for Him. The soul was never meant to lead us in life, but I didn't know that. Consequently, I got into occult practices as a way to find truth which, of course, did not work. The only truth is Truth Himself, Jesus Christ. Anyway, as my soul led this expedition, the Lord knew what I was doing. By His grace, He slowly but surely began drawing me to Himself, letting me know He saw me, knew my pain, and loved me. I firmly believe His Spirit (the Holy Spirit) was communicating to my spirit, even though I was DOA.

Your spirit (like mine) may be down but not out. The relationship God intended you to have with Him may be broken. You still have a spirit, but is it disconnected from God? If so, it is the "God piece" in you that is broken and cannot accomplish its intended purpose.

And this God piece needs to be called back to life!

God's passion is for you to be a spiritual person first. He wants you to have a spirit that is bigger than your soul, bringing the best out of your soul and body in this thing called life.

I believe God was calling me, whispering to me, and dropping His "love notes" into my innermost being many years before I accepted Jesus Christ as my Lord and Savior. It was like I was frozen deep inside, until the Spirit of God slowly warmed me up and thawed me out so I would accept Him. When I did, my spirit sprang to life!

You Need More than a Blessing

As a therapist, I came to understand the strong relationship between a person's thoughts, attitudes, and feelings. Thoughts and attitudes, sometimes undetectable at first, always precede feelings. It's easy to see how they can become a downhill path in a person's mind, because a person thinks the same way month after month, year after year. Little effort is required, and most folks are happy to operate this way. For healthy, balanced thinking, this is not a bad thing. But negative mindsets also follow this pattern, becoming impenetrable fortresses that are impervious to change. The Christian word for this phenomenon is "stronghold," a mindset developed and impregnated with hopelessness which is altogether invisible and resistant to change.

Before receiving the blessing, I was caught inside such a stronghold. There was shame and defectiveness in me, but I didn't know it. I had come to believe I was illegitimate and unworthy of God's love. God's Word penetrated my spirit, exposing the pain God was so ready to heal. "For the word of God is living and active. Sharper than any double-edged sword, it penetrates even to dividing soul and spirit, joints and marrow; it judges the thoughts and attitudes of the heart" (Hebrews 4:12). I was willed into existence by God. I was not a mistake! Hallelujah!

To know you are loved by God brings a great sense of peace into your life. When you receive His love in your spirit, you don't just think God loves you and you're acceptable; you know it. This is not based on emotion or circumstances. It is the truth. The Holy Spirit's main job is to speak God's love and truth to you. This brings great life! The Word of God supports this: "The Spirit Himself bears witness with our spirit that we are God's children" (Romans 8:16 NIV).

Be careful to note that this is not just a good feeling. You are made by God to respond to truth, not emotion. When the Spirit of truth communicates to your spirit, you believe it and never forget it. The blessing nurtures your spirit with the knowledge that you are made in God's image and when He made you, He was pleased! The more your spirit is nurtured this way, the more legitimate you feel. You begin to know and believe you are in the right place at the right time doing the right thing. You've got God's love in the most vital part of your being. There is no substitute for that.

All this is great, huge, and good ... but you need more than a blessing.

Divine Birthright

Your birthright is who you are and who God made you to be. It is your design by God.

Think about it—knowing your true identity and purpose affects everything. It determines which way you will go in life, how long it will take you to get there, and most importantly, whether or not you will experience true fulfillment.

As a child, you may have experienced a deep sense of injustice. Your birthright may have been stolen, although not intentionally, by any one person or persons, or lost because you were never told who you were in God's eyes. You were never told who He made you to be. In our culture, this is unfortunately the norm. Many forces conspire to separate you from knowing who you are.

Children need to be spiritually nurtured—told who they are and told about the potential God's placed inside them. In most homes this is not done. Children are left to find their identity for themselves. In a home with no father figure, for example, or where there's been emotional and/or physical abuse of any kind, children do well to survive, much less grow up with a sense of their God-given identity and purpose. For the children in a more stable environment, learning who they are oftentimes comes more from what others need them to be rather than who God made them to be.

The good news is, whatever your age, you can still learn to recognize your birthright and begin living out of your design in God. Your life will begin to make sense because you will see your purpose in living, and you will be better able to create stronger, richer, more life-giving relationships with others. It is God's desire to bless you so you may be a blessing to others.

There is a process of deep communication God wants to have with you. A word picture in Psalm 42:7 expresses this beautifully: "Deep calls to deep in the roar of your waterfalls; all your waves and breakers have swept over me." I believe the Spirit of God is trying to break through the static of your life to communicate His love to you, so you will not only know who you are and who He made you to be, but also so you will choose (if you haven't already done so) to accept Him as your personal Lord and Savior.

In the next chapter I share my story, in the hope it will help you recognize the process God may have you in. Could it be that God's Spirit has already been communicating with your spirit, but until now you've had no grid for it?

Chapter 2

The Search for Legitimacy

"THIS TEACHING *has been absolutely transforming. I grew up being taught (whether directly or indirectly) a very legalistic view of God and who He made us to be. The words "spirit" and "soul" were used interchangeably as if the same thing, and there was certainly no teaching on nurturing the spirit. Since sitting under this teaching, I have found the thing my spirit was longing for, although I never really knew what it was I was longing for.*

"A quote from a movie says it best. It's truly 'everything I never knew I always wanted.' My primary redemptive gift is Prophet and second is Exhorter. I never understood why I saw things or reacted to certain things the way I did. Sometimes I even felt like I was messed up somehow. When I did the survey and read the characteristics of my particular redemptive gifts, it was like someone had been following and studying me my whole life! Suddenly it all made sense. I'm not messed up! I'm exactly the way God created me to be.

"That revelation alone is priceless. I don't know what I would have done had I not learned the teachings on nurturing the spirit. The knowledge, tools, and confidence I have today as a result are immeasurable in worth."

— Ministry Leader

I graduated from a private women's college in Virginia; interned at the prestigious Johns Hopkins Hospital in

Baltimore, Maryland; worked at Cambridge University Press (the oldest Bible publisher in the world) in New York City; got a master's degree in counseling from the University of Alabama; rode horseback in Wyoming's Teton Mountains (at the age of thirty); among many other things. These are all amazing experiences for a person to have, yet after having done all these great things, I still did not feel legitimate.

In fact, I felt ashamed.

Shame, the opposite of legitimacy, was hidden from me. I didn't know it was inside me. This miserable, floating feeling had grown slowly over time, the result of painful experiences I had had and my wrong reactions to them. I had developed a mindset impregnated with hopelessness that was hidden from everyone, including myself.

I had parents, family, and friends who loved me, but at the deepest level of my being I felt unworthy and inadequate. Over time, as I pretended to feel good about myself and learned to stress and strain toward outward goals and achievements, as well as other people's approval, I began to wear down. The striving began to take its toll. I felt confused about who I was and what I could expect from others. I had no source of godly wisdom, although I'd been brought up in church. The things I'd learned about God, myself, and other people had come mostly from my family and peers. I felt a strong inner pressure to perform. I had totally bought into these values. I was driving myself to my own destruction.

It was Christmastime 1991—a dark stretch on my journey. I had let the stress in my life build to such a point that I felt I could not go on. I had gotten very down, but I was not out. On the day I thought I would be better off dead, I experienced a strength within me that absolutely refused to accept that lie. Strength came forth from the deepest part of me, my spirit. I responded to the Holy Spirit, Who told me to choose life, and by God's grace I did!

You may be thinking, *Huh? What happened?* This is what

happened: I distinctly heard the words "Choose life!" rise up from deep inside me (like an audible voice but not quite). Later, I learned that the words I heard were from Deuteronomy 30:19: "This day I call heaven and earth as witnesses against you that I have set before you life and death, blessings and curses. Now choose life, so that you and your children may live" (NIV). I had no knowledge of the Word of God at that time. What I do know now is the Spirit of God spoke truth to my spirit that day. The result? I felt God's love deep within me. He is the truth and He is love. When He speaks the truth in love to your spirit, you never forget it. Now I know God designed me to receive His love (from which my most fundamental sense of legitimacy comes) and truth in my spirit. He knew I would receive truth, reject death, and choose life on that day.

Fierce Intention—the Mark of the Human Spirit

I began to walk toward healing that day. The fierce intentionality, characteristic of an awakened human spirit, sprang to life inside me. Still, my faith in the Lord was pretty puny. Even though I'd grown up in church, I didn't know what prayer was, how to do it, or what it meant. I had no knowledge of the Word of God either. Mine was a mustard seed of faith; no more. But that's all God needs. By His grace I stepped out with my mustard seed. I had to believe life was more than it had been for me up to that point. I had gone to the top and back down again. Something had to give.

To God's glory, I still had a distinct impression in my inner being of how I felt and looked at life before all the lies of the enemy began to take hold (before I began to think I was "less than" for one reason or another). The impression was of a big-spirited person, one with a big deposit. Later I learned that God called me to be salt and light, to be a witness of His transforming power, and to show others what He's like. I knew I was both. God had been calling me all my life, but I had chosen the love (really fear) of people over the love of my Father.

A Slow Ramp-Up

I sought help and learned I had probably been depressed since childhood. My nervous system needed repair. I was thirty-one years old. That's how long it took for me to come to the end of myself. I took medication and hoped for the best. The doctor said repair could take a couple of years, after which medication might no longer be necessary. I quit my job with no job to go to—the first time in my life I'd ever done that. I borrowed money to bridge the gap and marched on.

I was a licensed professional counselor, so I started looking for a way to practice to bring some money in. That came pretty quickly. I now realize that was God's grace. I grabbed a position in a group counseling practice and not long after, I met my husband. More grace. Grace just started falling on me. And all the while I had this deep sense God was compensating me in some way. I would not have dared utter this to anyone, especially after all the ways I'd screwed things up in my life. That idea went against everything I had been taught to believe about life, and even about God. My thinking at that time was very simple: I'd screwed up; it was time to take my medicine and that was that, period. But God began to move in my life in a way only He can do; He began to bring healing to my spirit!

I kept myself in counseling and it helped some. I even dragged my sweet husband in with me, but for the most part, it was to watch and listen while two counselors (the therapist and I) analyzed and strategized about how to make things better. This wasn't all bad. In fact, God used the mouth of that counselor to send messages to my spirit (you know something has "landed" in your spirit when you remember it immediately and never forget it). One such powerful statement was, "For those who want to save their life will lose it, and those who lose their life for my sake will find it" (Matthew 16:25 NRSV). I really didn't get it at the time; it seemed so upside-down to me, but my spirit absolutely got it. I felt deeply affirmed and validated. The truth was spoken, my spirit recognized it, and more freedom came. I could not deny the fact that I had been holding onto my life for years, and the results were pretty close to disastrous.

Salvation. My Spirit Is Alive!

Later, my husband and I both made a commitment to a personal relationship with Jesus Christ. We did this together, and we were also baptized together. Amazing grace! I understand now, more than I did then, about the significance of this choice, and I am so glad we made it together. Because of the fall of man in the Garden of Eden, my spirit was separated from fellowship with God. I didn't really think God wanted to bother with me, have a personal relationship with me, or be personal to me in any way. My spiritual connection to true life (which is Him) was broken. When I accepted Jesus' atonement for my sin, my surrender to Him didn't just save me from everlasting condemnation (hell), but it restored true spiritual life to me here on earth in Him!

You may be wondering about the communication God made with my spirit before I was saved. That's where you see God's amazing grace and mercy toward you. His Word tells you that before you were in your mother's womb, He knew you: "Before I formed you in the womb I knew you, before you were born I set you apart; I appointed you as a prophet to the nations" (Jeremiah 1:5) and, "Your eyes saw my unformed body. All the days ordained for me were written in your book before one of them came to be" (Psalm 139:16). That is the Word of God, and it is true for you, whether your spirit has been brought back to life by accepting the blood of Jesus or not. "Your word, O Lord, is eternal; it stands firm in the heavens" (Psalm 119: 89). Believe it or not.

God knows you and God knows me. He is omniscient, omnipotent, and omnipresent. He knows everything that's going to happen in our lives, how we'll be sinned against by others, and how we'll sin against others before anything ever happens.

Even more astounding is the promise that "his divine power has given us everything we need for a godly life through our knowledge of him who called us by his own glory and goodness" (II Peter 1:3).

The Word of God applies to you. He knows it all and then brings His mercy and grace to bear on your life because He is seeking to draw you to Himself. He works to woo and awaken you to Him, even when your spirit is dead! The Holy Spirit stirs your spirit to thirst for and seek God. "But God is so rich in mercy, and he loved us so much, that even though we were dead because of our sins, he gave us life when he raised Christ from the dead. (It is only by God's grace that you have been saved!)" (Ephesians 2:4 NLT). This is love. This is God.

> ➤ *The importance of getting the knowledge of God into your spirit can't be understated. It applies not only to those who don't know Him, but certainly also to those who have come to repentance and belief in Jesus Christ. To take hold of Jesus in your innermost being is to live the abundant life He died to give you.*

Peace of Mind. Peace in Your Spirit

There is a blessing from the book *Blessing Your Spirit* by Arthur Burk and Sylvia Gunter that speaks to your spirit about being a sanctuary, not a war zone (as the latter, unfortunately, most of ours are). God's will is for the deepest part of your being to be a place of refuge in Him. Your inner life is then ordered and peaceful, just like Jesus'.

As I look back, I can see that many things blocked me from this peace, even while still in my mother's womb. As a child, I longed for peace of mind. I remember writing the phrase "peace of mind" on a piece of paper once. I don't think I'd ever heard anyone mention it. Likely I knew I would be laughed at for being so serious, so I chose not to expose my thoughts to anyone, but from somewhere deep inside I knew I wanted peace, and I definitely needed it.

Do you need peace? I believe your spirit is crying out for it.

What do you keep reaching for but never finding? What are you thirsting for? What lies have you believed and been telling yourself? What glass ceiling do you keep bumping up against? What is that big thing inside you that you have no idea how to get to, much less express? What past hurt keeps tripping you up just when you think you've got it all worked out? All these questions point to your spirit and God's unique design of you.

The answers come from Him and are inside you!

This may sound like just another Christian testimony to you, but there is something different here. Keep in mind that even the strongest rejection of Jesus (e.g. the apostle Paul, who violently persecuted believers in the early church) cannot keep Him from apprehending you. You've heard that before too, I'm sure. A person battles for years with the Lord, finally surrendering to Him and letting Him win him over.

I was one of them.

I finally surrendered at age thirty-eight, and then recognized my spirit had been crying out for Jesus my whole life! The deepest part of my being, the part God created to receive His love and purpose for my life, had been held captive for a very long time. When I accepted the Lord, my spirit was alive but still impoverished—worn down from years of ignorance and neglect, receiving little or no spiritual nourishment. What had I been doing all those years? I had been chasing fantasies of Jesus, looking for truth in tarot cards, I Ching, and runes (all occultic oracles); inner healing from New Age concepts; and practices and personal growth through the psychology of human reasoning. It was now time to follow God's order, to do what was necessary to position my spirit to lead!

To Follow God's Order—What Does That Mean?

God's order, His divine design, is found in this: "May God himself, the God of peace, sanctify you through and through. May your whole spirit, soul and body be kept blameless at the coming of our Lord Jesus Christ. The one who calls you is faithful, and he will do it" (I Thessalonians 5:23-24).

You don't have to be saved to have your spirit nurtured by God. He is so loving, merciful, and kind that He loves us and nurtures us whether we accept Him or not. His aim is to have deep intimacy with each one of us through His Son. That, however, is something that can only come when we have allowed His Spirit to regenerate our spirit through the blood of Jesus. Our spirits are then alive and able to experience deep communion with Him.

As I have shared, God was drawing me to Him, watching over and nurturing my spirit many years before I surrendered to His will and accepted Jesus Christ as my personal Lord and Savior. We are all saved through His grace by our faith. This can be a little difficult to understand, so here's God's Word to make it clearer: "Saving is all His idea, and all His work. All we do is trust him enough to let him do it. It's God's gift from start to finish! We don't play the major role. If we did, we'd probably go around bragging that we'd done the whole thing!" (Ephesians 2:8-9 MSG)

Our faith, remember, doesn't have to be any bigger than a mustard seed. It's not about our faith; it is about His amazing grace.

Chapter 3

Positioning Your Spirit to Lead

"MY GRANDSON *had been waking up a little past midnight crying and crying, and couldn't seem to console himself enough to get back to sleep. This had gone on for several nights, and it would take one of his parents a couple of hours to get him back to sleep. His father asked me if I knew of anything that would help. My immediate answer was that sometimes babies just go through these phases. Later on that night I was praying that my grandson and his parents would be blessed with a good night's rest. During my prayer time, the Lord told me to look in the pink book [Joy—see Appendix B] for a nighttime blessing.*

"The next day, as soon as my grandson took his nap, I went through the book. I found the right blessing! I told my son to go into my grandson's room, take dominion over the atmosphere, and cast out any spirits of unrest, bad dreams, etc. in the name of Jesus; then he was to bless my grandson with the blessing I had found before putting him to sleep for the night. My grandson slept until 5:30 the next morning! No sleep interruptions! And the restful sleep continues.

"I have learned so much! The power of nurturing our/others' spirits is incredible. I have experienced freedom from illegitimacy and opened my spiritual eyes to my legitimacy that can only be found in Him."

—Renee A.

"IN OUR *recent staff meeting, I was asked at the last moment to pray for one of our staffers who was going to Afghanistan for a year. Needless to say, I shuddered, but I knew God was in my presence because my coworker and I had been in His presence earlier that morning. I can truly say that God used me this morning to minister to the group through prayer. I am still on a godly high. Many were tearful afterwards. I am truly a blessed person. Spiritual nurturing has taught me numerous things. Dorinda is doing a great job."*

— *B. Cleveland*

"WHEN I *first held my three-month-old month old grandson in my arms and called his spirit to attention 'in the name of Jesus,' he immediately turned his head toward me and locked eyes on mine for the first time. As I proceeded to bless his spirit, he became very peaceful, yet attentive and outwardly happy. We continued this daily, and eight years later we still have this bond. At 6-8 months we began to go to my car every day, at his request, and listen to the "Blessing Your Spirit" CDs, as well as "The Father's Love" CD. This continued for several years. My experience with our second grandson is not the same, but we are very close, and I am his go-to guy with questions about God. I am more than convinced that long before we could understand each other in our souls, that both of these boys and I were communicating in our spirits, and because of that they have an understanding of God, the Spirit, that has changed their lives!"*

— *B. Trick*

"But the time is coming—it has, in fact, come—when what you're called will not matter and where you go to worship will not matter. It's who you are and the way you live that count before God. Your worship must engage your spirit in the pursuit of truth. That's the kind of people the Father is out looking for: those who are simply and honestly themselves before Him in their worship. God is sheer being itself—Spirit. Those who worship him must do it out of their very being, their spirits, their true selves, in adoration" (John 4:23-24 MSG).

When your spirit gets acknowledged and blessed, it is a game changer. But God doesn't want you to stop there. He wants you to gain a greater understanding of how He specifically made you. You need a sharper focus on the shape of your own spirit in order to accept yourself (finally) and accept the special way God's made you to receive His love. You see, even our "God receptors" are different from one another's. So if you've been comparing yourself with somebody else who may be designed quite differently than you, you've not only been doing yourself a disservice, but you have been limiting God's communication with you!

Your true self, your spirit, is the part of you God wants to have a primary relationship with. This book is one thing God may use to restore that relationship. This is spirit-to-spirit life, the way we were supposed to live with Him before our spirits died (as a result of the fall).

∽

The Redemptive Gifts of God

You are a reflection of God. He is sevenfold in spirit and so are you, because you are made in His image. When looking at your spiritual identity, you look at yourself and the designed life you came into this world with. It is your redemptive gift. Romans 12:6-8 spells out these gifts or aspects of God's nature inside you: "We have different gifts, according to the grace given us. If a man's gift is prophesying, let him use it in proportion to his faith. If it is serving, let him serve; if it is teaching, let him teach; if it is encouraging, let him encourage; if it is contributing to the needs of others, let him give generously; if it is leadership, let him govern diligently; if it is showing mercy, let him do it cheerfully." Prophet, Servant, Teacher, Exhorter, Giver, Ruler, and Mercy—these are the seven redemptive gifts of God. You, as an image bearer of God, possess all seven gifts, but there is usually one gift you identify with more than others.

This gift reflects God's nature in you. It is your spiritual identity and it is redemptive.

Redemptive?

The word "redeem" means to deliver, buy back, or reclaim. Anything redemptive redeems. God has made your very identity redemptive in order to heal you and make you whole, as well as to release His power in the earth through your life.

God creates everything for a purpose, including you. Your spiritual identity (redemptive gift) serves Him and serves you! As you move into greater understanding and acceptance of God's design of you, you will see His agenda. You will begin recognizing and receiving God's love in your life—His fingerprints—and as you do, you will experience fulfillment while fulfilling His plan for you.

I had no way of knowing all those years ago that God had deposited in me the spiritual DNA of the redemptive gift of Mercy.

Mercys are made to "be," not "do," and on the day I thought I would be better off dead, I was suicidal, in large part, due to exhaustion from all my *doing* to be okay in life. I had worn myself out trying to be someone I was never meant to be.

Understanding God's unique design has helped me release many harsh expectations and unrealistic demands I'd placed on myself (and others) that led to that episode of severe depression. As I learned about my primary redemptive gifts—Mercy and Prophet—my life began to make sense. The redemptive gift of Mercy is made to know God's heart. The redemptive gift of Prophet is made to know God's mind. The Mercy is slow to change, needing time to work through thoughts and feelings about a situation. The Prophet shifts gears quickly and tends to place a higher value on truth than relationships. I've come to see that it wasn't just a fluke, or even my idea alone, but God's design of me that led me to become a professional counselor.

It didn't take long for me to recognize that these polar opposite gifts (Mercy and Prophet) had made for some pretty challenging experiences in my life. What really made the difference was now I had a grid for what had been going on inside me and why peace had been so elusive. Just knowing God made me this way (I wasn't crazy) was a huge relief and a reason for hope.

$$\backsim$$

The following chapters detail the seven redemptive gifts of God. As you begin to look at these designs, you will recognize yourself in them. You will see that there may be many ways others can know you, but the most important knowing of who you are comes from God.

You may have experienced the pain and frustration of bringing your best to the table, only to find it wasn't good enough. If you don't know who you are and who God made you to be, you can spend years, decades, or a whole lifetime struggling to change what God has hardwired into your being. Gaining insight into why God made you helps you to understand and accept yourself (and others) and gives you the freedom to be who you are, not who someone else needs you to be.

> *Takeaway: Learn how very vital it is to nurture your spirit with the truth of who God says you are, how He designed you, and what He has made you to do!*

Coming to an understanding of the problems God designed you to solve releases you from solving problems He simply didn't design you to solve. [See Appendix A for the Redemptive Gifts Questionnaire.]

Each gift comes with a list of behavioral characteristics seen in people with that gift. Read it carefully, giving yourself time to recognize characteristics belonging to you. Each one of us portrays a unique reflection of God. You will likely agree with some of the characteristics belonging to each gift. This is because, again, we are all made in the image of God. He is sevenfold in spirit and so are we, so you may have a little or a lot of Prophet, Servant, Teacher, Exhorter, Giver, Ruler, and Mercy inside you. Don't sweat it. This is normal. As you read the behavioral characteristics, birthright, and battlefield for each gift, you will be moving from head knowledge to practical application.

Notice too that each of the seven gifts parallels a different day of creation. Based on what God did and/or created on each day, we see a vivid picture of the design and authority given to each gift.

You'll find a blessing at the end of each chapter for that particular gift. Read it aloud to your spirit. Strong encouragement and strength will come when you receive God's validation in this way.

(The material in the following chapters on the redemptive gifts comes from *Designed for Fulfillment – A Study of the Redemptive Gifts* by Charles Wale Jr. and was published by Arsenal Books, www.arsenalbooks.com.)

Chapter 4

The Redemptive Gift of Prophet

"STUDYING ALL *the redemptive gifts allows insight into how the body of Christ may best work together. Knowing my gift is Prophet allows me to offer my strengths to others, while reaching out for help and encouragement in my weaknesses. Recognizing the way God has made each of us strong in a different way results in effective organization for the army of the kingdom of God."*

— F. Edwards

"I HAVE *learned more about my spirit from Dorinda than from any other teacher. This has become a foundation of understanding concerning my spirit and its needs. Everybody needs this!"*

— K. Knight

"THE TEACHING *on the redemptive gifts was very affirming for me. It clarified some qualities I could see in myself—some positive and some which are challenges. I can now better understand that God has designed me with certain gifts and qualities He chose so I could accomplish the plans and purposes God has for me. I felt energized by the redemptive gifts teaching. It reminds me of Psalm 139 that says we are each fearfully and wonderfully made."*

— S. Goertz

Behavioral Characteristics

STRONG PERSONALITY	very opinionated
	thinks he is right and usually is
	a fast thinker
	tends to have a rather simplistic worldview—things are either good or bad, black or white
	offers his opinion whether you've asked for it or not
INTENSELY EMOTIONAL	has the widest range of emotions
	reacts strongly to things that are wrong, sinful, and painful
	driven to complete openness and honesty hard on himself and others; despises hypocrisy, especially in leadership
PASSIONATE FOR GOD	wants to see God's restoring power overcome the damage sin has caused
	wants to celebrate what God has done
	tends to be called to a higher level of sacrifice than any of the other gifts
	goes through the silences of God so God can build a deeper root system of faith for future fruit
VISIONARY	sees things others can't see
	vision is everything; cannot not go somewhere dead-end situations are
	needs a reason to live, a purpose to move toward needs to make sense out of everything
	knows the mind of God
	hears God's mind and speaks his mind over persons and situations
	the core value is to make something

new, to make something out of nothing

holds truth very tightly

prefers truth over relationship building

may appear cold and unfeeling

"out of sight, out of mind" attitude

fiercely competitive

rebuilder in the kingdom of God

solves problems

identifies and embraces problems and applies the right principle from God's Word to bring correction, restoration, and life

The Prophet in Scripture

Life is very simple for the Prophet who is bold and fearless, not one to mince words but one who is passionate to defend the reputation of God. Elijah was such a man.

Elijah challenged the people:
"How long are you going to sit on the fence?
If God is the real God, follow him;
if it's Baal, follow him. Make up your minds!"
Nobody said a word; nobody made a move.

Then Elijah said,
"I'm the only prophet of God left in Israel;
and there are 450 prophets of Baal.
Let the Baal prophets bring up two oxen;
let them pick one, butcher it,
and lay it out on an altar on firewood—but don't ignite it.
I'll take the other ox, cut it up,
and lay it on the wood. But neither will I light the fire.
Then you pray to your gods and I'll pray to God.
The god who answers with fire will prove to be,
in fact, God."

I Kings 18:21-24

Prophet Application

1. You crave the challenge of solving problems, and the wisdom of God is revealed when you do.

2. You want to make something new, do something new, and move forward toward "the new" continually. As on the first day of creation when God spoke creation into being, your spiritual DNA is to create something out of nothing.

3. The principle found in Matthew 6:33 has strong application for you: "But seek first his kingdom and his righteousness, and all these things will be given to you as well." You will suffer if you fail to give God the firstfruits of your time. You are called to a higher level of sacrifice than other people, which is for developing a strong root system in the Lord. Taking control of your time makes this happen.

4. You are passionate, intense, and sometimes mistake yourself for God, but you must come to grips with the fact that He doesn't have to have you to get the job done. He wants you to draw honor and glory to Him through the process He works in you and through you.

5. When you are a Prophet, it is impossible for you to not see what's going on around you, and you see things others can't see. It takes no time at all for you to see what's wrong in a situation, but God has called you beyond criticism in order to put truth to work to rebuild a life.

6. You are drawn to what's broken because God made you to see the devastation of sin. You know the fullness of His grace to restore. There are two groups of people you like to help: Leaders who take their role as leaders seriously, and those who are so broken they have lost hope for a life of dignity.

The Birthright and Battlefield for the Redemptive Gift of Prophet

Your birthright is who you are and who God made you to

be. For the redemptive gift of Prophet, it's all about providing vision to others about God's perspective of their lives—how He sees them, how He made them, and what He has called them to do. The Prophet needs to take hold of God's design. There will be times and seasons in the life of the Prophet when things are out of order, painful, and wrong. It is at these times the Prophet must learn to accept the pain and learn to see the redemptive purpose God has in even the most unrighteous situations.

My primary redemptive gift is Mercy, but I do score evenly with the redemptive gift of Prophet (see Questionnaire/Appendix A), so I've been known to get really hung up on what is right and wrong in a situation. I can become very critical of myself and others when things don't add up to my view of "right." As a believer in Christ, I am learning to recognize that, despite the whopping amount of sin and pain this world can dish up, God is in no way off His throne, nor has He decided to take a vacation day and leave me alone. His Word remains true despite my circumstances. Hebrews 13:5b brings powerful reassurance to me: "He |God| Himself has said, I will not in any way fail you nor give you up nor leave you without support. |I will| not, |I will| not, |I will| not in any degree leave you helpless nor forsake nor let |you| down (relax My hold on you)! |Assuredly not!|'" (AMP).

Trouble comes when I fear God is not in control and my life is just a random thing. This is a lie from the pit of hell. Unfortunately, most people have bought into this deception. God is in control of all our lives. How so? He is sovereign. "On his robe and thigh was written this title: King of all kings and Lord of all lords" (Revelation 19:16 NLT). There's ample evidence bad things happen to good people. Man is good at making a mess of his life, no thanks to God, the devil, or anyone else. But God is not to blame.

When I fell apart twenty years ago, somehow deep inside (my spirit) I got that. I knew I had made some big mistakes, but somehow I also knew God loved me and He was going to make things right. I understand better now that God takes the pain that comes into our lives (by our own hands or the hands of others) and transforms it into good things before the end of the story of our lives. Prophets need to know and recognize that suffering positions us to receive more deeply from God. If I hadn't fallen apart, I likely would have continued depending on myself; I would have continued feeling illegitimate (but never knowing it) and searching and searching for Jesus, possibly never choosing to trust in Him for my life.

As a professional counselor, I help people solve problems. True to my design, I hate dead-end situations and want to make sense of everything. I try to help people find the good in the bad they are going through. As you can imagine, this can be a pretty hard sell and, as anyone who's lived any amount of time can tell you, there are some problems that just don't get solved. This is a critical time for the Prophet to know who God is, and who he is in Him, so he can resist the devil's lie that something is wrong with him or what he's done.

God calls the redemptive gift of Prophet to be a rebuilder and restorer of what is broken down and chaotic. Isaiah 58:12 describes it eloquently: "Your people will rebuild the ancient ruins and will raise up the age-old foundations; you will be called Repairer of Broken Walls, Restorer of Streets with Dwellings."

And this brings us to the battlefield for the Prophet. The battle is to live according to God's design (taking principles from God's Word and finding new tools for rebuilding and healing) vs. choosing to exit relationships when people disappoint you, and they will disappoint you.

There are many situations in life in which the Prophet's fondness for honesty, transparency, high character, and decisiveness will be met with less than an enthusiastic response.

This can be agony for the Prophet, who doesn't understand why others aren't motivated to solve the problems the Prophet finds so obvious.

The resulting disconnect is a frustrating and lonely place for the Prophet to be. It is a place the devil takes advantage of in order to work his agenda (John 10:10—to kill, steal, and destroy), resulting many times in the Prophet's decision to just go it alone.

But this is not God's best. The power for redemption comes when the Prophet chooses to remain in relationship despite the pain, loss, sorrow, etc., all the while keeping his eye on God and on what God is doing to release His power in the earth. Prophets need to learn to stay in the game, rejecting judgment and bitterness when others don't live up to their high standards. They also need to watch that they don't become holier-than-thou people nobody wants to get close to. When that happens, the devil wins again.

The Prophet carries life-giving insight, but it will go nowhere if no one wants to get close enough to receive what he has.

A Prophet must also resist taking things into his own hands when the going gets tough. If he doesn't, he will regret it. God is not mocked. What we sow, we reap. The Prophet must allow God to be the problem solver, letting God show the way toward His blessing.

God's desire for the Prophet is to partner with Him to solve problems, not follow his own agenda. This is dominion thinking—partnering with God to do His will in His time. This alone brings true fulfillment.

Prophet Blessing

Beloved, I call your spirit to attention in the name of Jesus Christ of Nazareth. I bless and celebrate the Prophet portion of who you are. Prophet, you occupy a special place because you are the first of the seven redemptive gifts found in the human spirit. Your gift is to provide vision to others so they can possess their birthrights in God.

You are made to be fearless, to walk in bold faith in the principles found in the Word of God. Your essence is light, a distinct wavelength of God's light. You are one who is not intimidated by the unknown. Just as God spoke light into existence on the first day of creation, so you are made to see the light of God and speak it into the darkness of people's lives and situations.

God has made you a light-dweller, but you are not afraid to endure pain to get there. You may have lived through some pretty big darknesses in your own life—darkness that came as a result of abuse or neglect that may be compounded by the fact you were never introduced to your Father God. Regardless of the reason, I bless you with turning your attention to the face of your Father God. I bless you with turning the light of your spirit into the light of the Spirit of God. I bless you with allowing the light of God's Spirit to shine on your light, releasing you from your painful past and washing you clean by the power of the blood of Jesus. I bless you with knowing you are made in the image of Almighty God, and that when He made you, He judged you to be good.

I bless your passion and intensity as a "spiritual skyscraper" in the kingdom of God. You are called by God to be moving continually upward toward Him. You see things others can't see and move toward the new and uncharted territory God is calling you to. You thrill to God's voice as He calls you to spiritual peaks ahead. I bless you with knowing that even if things around you appear static and unchanging, life in the kingdom never stands still. I bless and celebrate the pioneer that you are—someone who is made by God to plow the hard ground of pain during personal transformation in a way that positions others to embrace their birthrights. I bless you with making the pain in your life and the lives of others productive for the kingdom of God.

Finally, I bless you, Prophet, with making the main thing the main thing in your walk with God. I bless you with knowing God is sovereign over your life and with recognizing the principles that apply to your intimacy with Him as the most critical truths for you to learn this side of heaven. I bless you with great fulfillment as you find God's love for you, first, and then pass it on as you lead others to Him. I bless you, Prophet, in Jesus' mighty name.

Chapter 5

The Redemptive Gift of Servant

"MANY TRAGIC *events took place in my life when I was young, so I spent four decades of my life convinced I had no ability to set boundaries. I had inadvertently transferred all of my life and God-given authority over to an illegitimate mindset of servitude. When I began discovering and nurturing the truth in my spirit, I was set free! I began to rewrite the story of my life, nurturing my spirit with the truth that is only in His words for me. As a Servant, I am free from the devil's boundaries and capable of setting boundaries of truth in Jesus."*

— R. T. Green

"THIS KNOWLEDGE *will help mold and mature me for the rest of my life. Unpacking each layer of my spirit and then repacking it in the most effective way glorifies God. I now have an excellent perspective of myself and others. Learning the dynamics of the different gifts has helped my relationships with family and friends blossom, my interaction with strangers become more personable, and my understanding of God's unconditional love deepen. The impressions on me have been life altering and will be everlasting."*

— L. Clark

Behavioral Characteristics

SUSTAINER OF LIFE	meets both the physical and spiritual needs of others but prefers to remain low profile is not comfortable with attention
PRACTICAL AND FLEXIBLE	a hard worker
	possesses a strong ability to recognize what needs doing now and does it, even to the detriment of his own health
LOYAL AND TRUE	entrusted by God to be an armor bearer who prays for leaders
	pure-hearted; does not seek his own agenda
	has been rewarded with great spiritual authority
LOVES THE UNLOVABLE	a "porcupine hugger"
	comes alongside deeply wounded people to show them God's grace and Mercy for healing
	has eyes of love for the hardest cases
ARMOR BEARER	cares for and ministers to leaders
	prays for restoration in families
	prays for the sick, especially in threatened premature death
	prays for nature, weather, and land
VICTIM MINDSET	has issues of self-worthlessness
	tends to tolerate indignity and shaming, especially in his family
	believes lies that cause him to feel inadequate for spiritual responsibilities or authority keeps peace at any cost
	will tell you why it's right for things to be wrong—the epitome of the victim mindset
TEAM PLAYER	sees the best in others

very, very loyal to family
totally trustworthy and reliable
has pure motives
straightforward, honest, and true
wants others to achieve their best
experiences the greatest fulfillment
when he knows he has helped someone

The Servant in Scripture

The Servant knows and protects her boundaries as she walks in childlike obedience to God. Queen Esther is just such an example of this gift.

"Then Esther again spoke to the king,
    falling at his feet, begging with tears
to counter the evil of Haman the Agagite
    and revoke the plan that he had plotted against the Jews.
The king extended his gold scepter to Esther.
    She got to her feet and stood before the king.
She said, "If it please the king and he regards me
    with favor and thinks this is right,
and if he has any affection for me at all,
    let an order be written that cancels the bulletins
authorizing the plan of Haman son of Hammedatha
    the Agagite to annihilate the Jews in all the king's provinces.
How can I stand to see this catastrophe wipe out my people?
    How can I bear to stand by
and watch the massacre of my own relatives?"

Esther 8:3-6

Servant Application

Your primary heart motivation is to see all things restored. This makes your prayers very precious in God's sight. You tend to be guileless—an individual who carries no ulterior motives—so when God speaks, you obey. He trusts you, but you can really struggle with trusting and respecting yourself.

In order to develop the spiritual identity and legitimacy God gave you, you must make a choice. You must choose to allow the Holy Spirit to grow you up. You must decide you are going to be fiercely intentional in positioning yourself for Him to do this. How? One way is by blessing your spirit every day aloud with the Word of God and its blessings.

You have been designed to have spiritual authority in the following areas:

1.   to comfort and care for leaders through practical assistance and prayer so they may enter into God's presence,

2.   to usher families into the kingdom of God (salvation, restoration, healing, deliverance),

3.   to come against the spirit of death, particularly in the case of premature death (read the book of Esther; she is your role model),

4.   to call forth restoration over land, buildings, and ecology.

5.   to seek God for other Servants who will join you to pray for leaders. Open your mind to praying for institutions outside the church.

Your weakness is to default to living like a victim. See yourself through God's eyes. He finds you trustworthy because you don't use the power He gives you for your own agenda. As you step up to the plate and do the things God's put in your heart to do, you'll be blessing others and yourself too. You'll gain spiritual muscle (authority) to bring the kingdom of God (righteousness, peace, and joy in the Holy Spirit) to earth.

Remember, the demonic is utterly secondary; it cannot take hold unless there is a mindset it can attach to. If there is no mindset, there is no legal right of the enemy to bring oppression. Continually renew your mind in the Word of God so you can walk in your calling. You have the mind of Christ.

The Birthright and Battlefield for the Redemptive Gift of Servant

When the Servant does what God designed him to do, he will be dangerous to the kingdom of darkness. He will be fulfilled in his life and be a life-giver to others, especially leaders. As the Servant quickly obeys God's voice, God trusts him to pray for leaders and for restoration in all things. God gives the Servant a greater impact in prayer, and this is based on his design and deep loyalty to God. The Servant's purpose is to advance God's kingdom values in the earth by releasing His cleansing and purifying power in all situations. Situations get restored, and people are healed and positioned to reach their destiny.

It's often surprising to watch the way a person with the redemptive gift of Servant responds in a situation. Watch one. You'll see he doesn't flinch, second-guess, analyze, or worry about stuff the way some other people do. He doesn't concern himself with implications and outcomes. He leaves it up to God to resolve those issues. He simply hears and obeys. He walks in childlike faith. This is God's gift to the Servant, and His gift to us who need help trusting God's leading voice.

It's not unusual for a Servant to grow up in a family in which he is dominated by others. This can be by parents, siblings, relatives, or all three. Later he may marry a dominating spouse or get a job with a boss who's a dominator. The devil works through these relationships and experiences to steal the Servant's sense of self-worth. Think about what you've read so far. Wouldn't you, if you were the devil, fight tooth and nail to keep that Servant deceived about who he is and who God made him to be (his birthright)?

Even when Servants see power being misused and abused, they rarely confront it. They may fail to recognize abuse because they are accustomed to thinking of themselves as "less than" and being treated the same way. They aim to keep peace at all costs. No problem for the dominators, who just keep on dominating, but this is not God's best for the Servant.

↩

So this brings us to the battlefield, which for the Servant is to walk in godly authority rather than with a victim mindset. The Servant must learn who he is and who God has made him to be. His place in the community of the human spirit is like no other. No other gift walks at such a high level of spiritual authority. It is a place of honor and dignity. Servants must stop allowing themselves to be controlled by others more than being controlled by God. They must fight to accept that their true identity and worth comes from Him.

Servants need to protect their boundaries around their time, talents, and relationships and not become a doormat for others to walk on. Only when the Servant learns to connect with God will he be able to give a godly no before he gives a hearty yes to the demands of others for support and assistance.

Jesus set a powerful example for us in this. During His time on earth He showed us that He responded to His Father, not the needs of man. There were many times He picked up and moved from a place where there were great needs to go on to the next assignment His Father had for Him. It didn't matter to Jesus when others didn't understand Him or even came against Him; His legitimacy was not based on their approval but on the love of His Father. He knew what His Father wanted Him to do and He did it. This is the kind of unshakeable security He wants for us, a rock-solid knowing that we are living inside the strength of His will for our lives.

↩

I've known some tremendous Servants in my time, but I didn't know it was a redemptive gift of God I was witnessing. Most of them were women breaking their backs to serve and meet the needs of the rest of us. It seemed they walked with an uncanny knack (others would call that an anointing from God) to know what was needed in a situation and provide it before anyone asked for it. Another indicator you are dealing with a gift God gives is there is life on it. You can tell the person loves to do what he is doing and he can't seem to stop doing it; he can't get enough! This is surely the case with the redemptive gift of Servant. He just goes from one thing to the next continuously. There are always needs to meet—spiritual, emotional, and physical—and the Servant stands ready to meet them.

Additional Points for Application:

• This may sound dramatic, but the battle truly is for the Servant's dignity. He must be established in godly authority.

• He has a great ability to meet needs and be a loyal team member, serving all kinds of leaders, but he can easily tip over into exhausting himself. He should establish a healthy, balanced lifestyle, set boundaries around his health and well-being, and protect it through good nutrition, exercise, rest, and fun.

• To develop his spiritual authority, he must feed his spirit. His spirit is the receptacle God designed for His love and legitimacy. The Servant can't walk in authority if he doesn't feel legitimate. Legitimacy comes first. Everything follows it. It is the groundwork for the rest of the spirit, soul, and body.

• He should call his spirit to attention to hear the truth of God's Word for him. This feeds and nurtures him and will bring him up. He will begin to feel more deserving of respectful treatment from others. He will learn how to train others how to treat him by demanding respect and rejecting dishonor. Jesus walked this way, and He expects us to do the same.

• Don't buy into the lie that helping other people succeed is what makes the Servant a worthwhile human being. This is a savior mentality. It can also set the Servant up to be victimized by others. Remember, the Servant's legitimacy comes from two things and two things only:

- God loves him.
- When He made him, He judged him as good!
- His worth does not come from serving people in this way; his worth comes from God and God alone. He must do what God tells him to do and let God build the success platforms for him and other people.

Servant Blessing

Beloved, I call the Servant portion of your spirit to attention in Jesus' name. Servant, I want to bless and celebrate you as the second of the redemptive gifts found in the human spirit. You are the portion of God's light He made to cleanse, support, and protect life—like the atmosphere and water of the second day of creation. This is who you are and who God made you to be. This is your birthright.

I bless you, Servant, with providing the atmosphere that sustains both physical and spiritual life. I bless your love and loyalty for your Father, God, which is the power that generates your spirit. You have a heart for Him, to serve Him, so you serve His sheep in physical and spiritual ways too. You delight to serve Him at His pleasure. His agenda is your agenda. I bless you with following God's agenda and the fulfillment this brings to you when you do.

I bless you, Servant, with accepting the greatness of your gift. You may have experienced abuse by which the enemy sought to delegitimize you. The assault may have been great, because your gift is great and he knows it. Still, I bless you, Servant, with recognizing your Father God is infinitely greater than your enemy. He knows full well what He has deposited in you. I bless you with receiving the authority He has entrusted you with. I bless you with responding obediently to the Spirit of God as He gives you assignments that will bring His restoring power into broken people and situations.

Servant, I bless you with possessing the spiritual authority to come against the power of death and, in particular, premature death. You have the redemptive gift of Queen Esther, who walked in spiritual authority over both physical and spiritual death. Like Esther, who stood against the potential extermination of all Israel, you stand in the gap for those who are perishing both spiritually and physically. You bring your great faith in God's goodness and faithfulness to bear on a crisis situation.

Servant, I bless you with receiving your legitimacy by receiving God's love and trusting in who He says you are, not in the definition given by the people or circumstances around you. Never has this been more vividly portrayed than when Jesus hung between two thieves on a cross: When the thief told Jesus to remember him when He came into His kingdom, Jesus said, "I tell you the truth, today you will be with me in paradise" (Luke 23:43). Despite the circumstances, Jesus knew who He was. The fact He was being crucified did not touch who He was or who His Father made Him to be. He possessed His birthright even as He hung on the cross! He knew He was the Lamb slain before the foundation of the world to redeem all mankind.

I bless you, Servant, with knowing deep in your spirit that you have been called to such a time as this. I bless you with allowing the Spirit of God to help you make peace with your past so you can begin to walk in high authority, partnering with your Father God to bring many sons and daughters into submission to His life-giving laws. In the name of Jesus Christ of Nazareth, I bless you.

Chapter 6

The Redemptive Gift of Teacher

"LEARNING ABOUT *my spiritual gifting and how it relates to every part of my being has impacted my life more deeply than I could have ever imagined. Knowing my primary gift is Teacher has allowed me to understand why I am drawn to research, and how sowing into the lives of others brings me great fulfillment.*

"Not only do I now know my strengths and have a newfound ability to step out in confidence, but I am also aware of the things that hinder me. Knowing what affects me negatively has given me the strength to act rather than react, changing each of my relationships for the better."

— S. Barnhard

"I RECOGNIZE *my legal right to partner with God and I am able to walk daily in the authority Christ died for me to possess.*

"I have been empowered to grow deeper in my relationship with the Holy Spirit. I now have the tools I need to truly possess my birthright. My birthright, who I am and who God made me to be, comes from my relationship with the Father, Son, and Holy Spirit."

— T. Sams

Behavioral Characteristics

LOVER OF TRUTH	pursuit of knowledge is at his core
	prefers doctrine and the established way of doing things over personal experience or revelation
	his biggest motivation is to validate the truth, to be sure truth is truth
GENERATIONAL GIFT	has a greater ability to produce fruit (teaching of the truth) that will feed generations to come (like the Giver and Ruler)
DETAIL ORIENTED	slow to respond to/receive new ideas
	thoughtful decision maker
	needs to see the end from the beginning
	can frustrate others who think he should move faster
	tends to get mired down in endless study and details
QUIET AND THOUGHTFUL	in demeanor
	others feel safe to come to him with their hurts
	a patient counselor who waits for people to make course corrections and reconcile themselves to God
	deeply committed to family and tradition
	a great sense of humor
PASSIVE	responsible on his own terms
	does not like telling others what their responsibilities are
	finds it hard to demand that others take responsibility
	tends to select the responsibility he will take on himself
	must resist passivity and impose

	responsibility on himself and others when this is the right thing to do
HEAD OVER HEART	prefers thinking to feeling
	tends to walk by sight and not by faith
	prefers doctrine over intimacy with God
	struggles with prayer and intimacy with God
ANCHOR FOR THE TRUTH	provides a stabilizing influence when serving with other more impulsive gifts

The Teacher in Scripture

Luke had to be sure you knew he knew what he was telling you was the truth. This compulsion is the essence of the redemptive gift of Teacher, who takes his responsibility as an accurate recorder of the truth very seriously.

In the fifteenth year of the rule of Caesar Tiberius—
      it was while Pontius Pilate was governor of Judea;
Herod, ruler of Galilee;
      his brother Philip, ruler of Iturea and Trachonitis;
Lysanias, ruler of Abilene;
      during the Chief-Priesthood of Annas and Caiaphas—
John, Zachariah's son, out in the desert at the time,
      received a message from God.
He went all through the country around the Jordan River
      preaching a baptism of life-change
leading to forgiveness of sins,
      as described in the words of Isaiah the prophet:
Thunder in the desert! "Prepare God's arrival!
      Make the road smooth and straight!
Every ditch will be filled in,
      Every bump smoothed out, The detours straightened out,
All the ruts paved over. Everyone will be there to see
      The parade of God's salvation."

Luke 3:1-6

Teacher Application

God has made you in such a way that you crave truth. You want more and more validation of it and more and more credentials as a result of studying it.

However, your spirit becomes dry when you focus in this direction too long. God wants to bring you into deep intimacy with Him through experiencing His manifest (clearly visible to the eye) presence.

God has supernatural strategies He wants to reveal to you as you bring His manifest presence to bear on the problems He presents you. (Your attitude should be: *I may not know how to solve this problem now, but I have the ability to solve this problem within me.*)

Begin by recognizing God's fingerprints on your life daily. Celebrate His goodness and mercies in your emotions. Get out of your head!

You have a tendency to take responsibility on your own terms. This is a religious mindset. God doesn't want your religious activity; He wants your heart. Listen with your spirit to Psalm 51: 16-17: "You do not delight in sacrifice, or I would bring it; you do not take pleasure in burnt offerings. The sacrifices of God are a broken spirit; a broken and contrite heart, O God, you will not despise."

You have been called to devote your family to God, to make them whole and set them apart for His purposes. Your family is your primary mission field and should be your first priority. God expects you to do what He wants in your family before you accept responsibility elsewhere.

The ultimate goal of truth is not the acquisition of knowledge but the celebration of the kingship of Jesus Christ. Your task is to develop intimacy with the Lord and worship Him, not just pile up knowledge and understanding. Call your spirit to attention to hear the word of the Lord: "When I tried to understand all this, it troubled me deeply till I entered the sanctuary of God" (Psalm 73:16-17).

The Birthright and Battlefield for the Redemptive Gift of Teacher

The birthright of the Teacher is to be that person who recognizes and knows God's deep truths, allows God to speak to him through experiences in life, and takes back to others (especially his family) the revelation of who God is. "If the truth leads us to Jesus, it has accomplished its purpose. But if the truth itself becomes the focal point, it is just another form of the knowledge of good and evil. Its fruit will be death, regardless of how true it is. The information found at the Tree of Knowledge may no doubt be true and factual, but there is truth that kills and there is the Truth who gives life—and we must learn to distinguish between them" (*There Were Two Trees in the Garden*, 2006, 57).

Teachers battle with making the pursuit of truth and religious activity the focal point, when the author of all truth is the One they should be looking for and seeking intimacy with. The devil insinuates his agenda to puff them up, to convince them their legitimacy comes from what they know and what they do. Their God-given design to crave truth in order to bring their family (and others) into wholeness gets derailed.

The Word of God speaks to this battle: "Such knowledge, however, puffs a person up with pride; but love builds up" (1 Corinthians 8:1 GNT). The New Living Translation puts it this way, "While knowledge makes us feel important, it is love that strengthens the church."

Recognize the subtlety of the religious spirit—it is always in pursuit of more activity, more knowledge, more anything outside of Jesus. We must wake up to the fact that the devil has distracted us too long. We must return our focus to the One Who embodies all truth and life. He alone is the Way.

So the birthright God is so passionate for the Teacher to receive and walk in is: Be that husband (wife), father (mother), minister, and leader who knows God's deep truths, knows Him experientially, and then reveals His presence to others.

At the end of the day, the question boils down to whether the Teacher will choose to respond to God or not, to walk as Jesus walked, bringing truth to bear in every situation and circumstance.

Additional Points for Application

• Do you know Jesus or do you just know about Him? God wants you to incarnate the person and character of Jesus, not just document Him.

• Going to the Word first is honorable and appropriate, but the best reflection of God's truth is incarnated in your life, not words or ideas.

• Identifying with Christ settles the issue of how valid or legitimate you are. Credentials and degrees are not your source of legitimacy in God.

• Giving your spirit the time, space, and solitude it needs to hear from the Lord—to know Him and what He wants you to do—is legitimate. Simplicity, solitude, silence, and prayer are four ingredients for developing intimacy with the Lord.

• Settling for knowledge and missing intimacy with God (through in-depth personal interaction) is a mistake you can easily make. Live in intimacy and worship by feeding both your spirit and your mind. Listen to the Word and the Spirit speaking to you and encouraging you, which is the best of both worlds—Spirit and truth!

• Patiently waiting for those in sin to become convicted and repent is one of your strengths, but be sensitive to God's voice when He says enough is enough, and the time for godly confrontation has come.

Teacher Blessing

I call the Teacher portion of your spirit to attention to receive God's blessing for you.

I bless you, Teacher, as you represent the powerful third day of creation, a day in which God released a whole new aspect of His nature into the world— the ability to convert and multiply. On this day God created the trees, herbs, and seed-bearing plants, and He created one of the greatest miracles of life— the process by which a seed is planted in the soil to then grow into a plant we use to sustain life.

I bless you, Teacher, with understanding your true identity and purpose. God has made you to be a source of understanding and stability in the body of Christ, and I bless that aspect of God's nature in you. I bless your vigorous pursuit of truth with a coinciding increase of faith to receive God's truth from outside your traditional go-to sources. I bless you with receiving truth from a blend of God's logos (scriptural truth) and rhema (revealed truth) to grow in intimacy and worship of Him, not simply accumulating more knowledge and doctrine.

The process of life from seed to plant is a picture of you, Teacher. I bless you with hearing God's call to be that part of the human spirit that speaks the seed of truth to the body of Christ. I bless you with bringing life, healing, and health as you speak the revitalizing truth of God's word into the soil of the lives He gives you.

I bless you,Teacher, for being a lover of truth. It is truth you crave and truth you live for, and I bless that as good. I bless you to remember that it is not the pursuit of truth that gives life but its application that releases God's power to heal and make whole. The seed must have soil to grow in, and you must learn how to sow seed that can be heard and received by many—many who may never darken the doors of a church to hear truth communicated in more traditional ways.

Teacher, I bless you with hearing the call of God to sanctify your family. This is the virtue you have been called to walk in, because you are made by God to know His deep truths in a profound way and to communicate them to the generations that follow. I bless you with knowing in the depths of your spirit that you carry a generational anointing and, because of that fact, there is a greater impact for good or evil based on what you do in your lifetime. I bless you with doing what God wants you to do with your birthright—to reveal His tangible presence to others to cause them to pursue Him for themselves. I bless you with doing this so well that your children crave the presence of God above all things. I bless you, Teacher, with establishing a legacy of physical and spiritual children who own their faith for themselves and who will reject religious activity where God is not present.

I bless you, Teacher, with all these mighty blessings. In the name of the living Truth Himself, Jesus Christ, I bless you.

Chapter 7

The Redemptive Gift of Exhorter

"THIS IS *the daily adventure of the Exhorter: Several years ago I met a single mother in the church parking lot. As she shared her dream to become a registered nurse, I shared with her that I saw her in a position far beyond that—that of a nurse practitioner. I prayed with her for courage, strength, and finances, reminding her that with God all things are possible. She called me six weeks later and told me she was enrolled in college. With much prayer and encouragement, she graduated from college as a registered nurse. She had a great job, but one day she texted me that she was going back to school to become a nurse practitioner. Glory to God!*

"As an Exhorter, I really believe deep down in my spirit all the promises of God are yes and amen! With the help of the Holy Spirit, our hearts are filled with encouraging, powerful words. As we speak, words change lives, words give life, words change destinies, words build."

— *V. Chadwick*

"EXHORTER—THAT'S ME! *I didn't know the way I interacted with people all along was a wonderful gift from God. This is my season to begin on the path the Lord has laid out for me. My cage has been opened to let my spirit soar!"*

— *J. Butler*

Behavioral Characteristics

WORLD CLASS BELIEVER	can cross all barriers to connect to all people
	is a visionary who sees the biggest picture, the largest number, etc.
	carries a big vision
	most world-changers are Exhorters— they have to be to do it!
PEOPLE ORIENTED	never meets a stranger
	enjoys the company of others
	his lightheartedness and ability to work a crowd makes him appear superficial, but he's not
	great team member and networker
GREAT COMMUNICATOR	shares his faith easily and in difficult situations
	teaches from personal experience
	helps others to see God in practical ways
STRONG PEACEMAKER	can disagree with others without losing relationship
	skilled at starting and keeping relationships, whatever the cost
	master reconciler
VERY FLEXIBLE	not intimidated by new ideas or truth
	likes to start things and move on
	a hard worker
	intensely busy
	does well with less sleep than most folks
	likes to have many projects going at one time
HEART SENSITIVE	recognizes others' feelings and the timeframe they need to come alongside a new idea

	sees spiritual lessons in personal pain and suffering
TRANSLATOR	for the heart of God
	gets to know God and then wants to communicate Him to others
	opens his own heart to open the hearts of others
POOR TIME MANAGEMENT	struggles with disciplining his time
	struggles to resist the tyranny of the urgent (things that are pressing for attention that are right in front of him) in order to accomplish higher goals
SENSITIVE TO REJECTION	especially from within the group
	must be willing to risk offense to obey God

The Exhorter in Scripture

The power to govern and give light is the essence of the beauty of the Exhorter, and is reflected in the following verses.

The heavens declare the glory of God;
    the skies proclaim the work of his hands.
Day after day they pour forth speech;
    night after night they reveal knowledge.
They have no speech, they use no words;
    no sound is heard from them.
Yet their voice goes out into all the earth,
    their words to the ends of the world.
In the heavens God has pitched a tent for the sun.

Psalm 19:1-4

And God said, "Let there be lights in the vault of the sky to separate the day from the night, and let them serve as signs to mark sacred times, and days and years, and let them be lights in the vault of the sky to give light on the earth." And it was so. God made two great lights—the greater light to govern the day and the lesser light to govern the night. He also made the stars. God set them in the vault of the sky to give light on the earth, to govern the day and the night, and to separate light from darkness. And God saw that it was good. And there was evening, and there was morning—the fourth day.

Genesis 1:14-20

Exhorter Application

1.   You are God's world changer. You carry the global heart of God for all people, as well as the gift of revealing Him to others.

2.   You have been given divine power to influence others through your relationship with them and to reconcile them to God.

3.   You are the one whose faith, vision, and relationship with God sheds light on Him and His ways. This brings others into deeper relationship with Him.

4.   You are made to bring the extraordinary light of God to others—a pure message from a pure heart. The sequence God wants you to follow is: Receive from Him first, then communicate Him to others.

5.   Sowing and reaping is a long-term endeavor and easily bypassed by the Exhorter. You can value comfort and quick results (denying the reality of what it takes to achieve God's best).

6.   Your easiest strength (inspiring, connecting, and mobilizing people) can become your greatest weakness if you are not submitted to God. You must be willing to stand for God alone, even if it means you may be rejected by others.

7.   Like Moses and Gideon, God calls you to know Him, to

know His nature. From that rock solid confidence in knowing who he is, you lead others to do His will. The issue is never about God's power, it is about knowing God's character.

The Birthright & Battlefield for the Redemptive Gift of Exhorter

Popular, winsome, friendly—the Exhorter—this is who he is and who God made him to be. What a birthright! He is known for his gift of the gab and ability to put people at ease. His lighthearted approach to living is joyful and contagious; he is open to what's happening in life. The birthright is right there, because God uses all these beautiful things to reveal Himself in order to draw people in. God gives the Exhorter a heart to share Him with others. The Exhorter helps people "see" God in a very real and practical way so they will choose to love Him and live for Him too.

I have a pastor who is a strong Exhorter. He is a wonderful communicator and one of the most inspiring people I know. I know he loves me, and I know he knows how I feel about things. He has an excitement for life and for the Lord that is truly contagious. Of course, everyone wants a piece of him, and this is where the battle lies—not just for my dear pastor, but for all Exhorters who want to live at their highest potential in God. They must choose to invest in their vertical relationship with God before investing in the horizontal relationships around them. When they follow God's divine order, everyone wins!

With every gift comes "free money." This refers to the empowerment that comes through God's design. We are made in God's image, and there is a particular portrait of Himself He wants to release through each of us; usually it's your easiest strength, perhaps the thing you can't get enough of. Some would call it anointing. It's something you don't have to work at. It comes naturally and gives life to other people. Remember the description of my pastor? He lives life based on his design. He knows who he is and what God's made him to do. He does it, and it is very life-giving to him and to me.

So "free money" is each person's easiest strength, but there is a deeper strength God has invested in our redemptive design. The Exhorter's easiest strength is his ability to make relational connections, but his deepest strength comes from the Word of God. Because our culture seeks comfort, pleasure, and excitement, the Exhorter can bow to his own and others' pressure to produce quick results. God calls the Exhorter to commit to long-term sowing and reaping in his relationship with Him and with other people.

This is the battle for the Exhorter—committing to long-term sowing and reaping for God's purposes vs. denying the reality of this principle and never achieving fulfillment.

Easy strength vs. deeper strength: the Exhorter must make the choice. Will he commit to long-term investment in his relationship with God and others, or go with a short-term investment that yields faster results? If he chooses the former, he is doing things God's way. Sowing that advances the kingdom of God requires a commitment to produce fruit that will last, and this takes time. However, if the Exhorter chooses the latter—the quick-fix route—the results will be a life lived at surface level: definitely not God's best for this tremendous gift.

God uses the redemptive gift of Exhorter to minister powerfully to others. Like the sun, moon, and stars God made on the fourth day of creation, the Exhorter is made to bring great light based on the revelation he receives from God. The Exhorter is made to give people knowledge of God, period.

More Points to Consider:

- We receive God's best when we submit to His ways. One

of His ways is the principle of sowing and reaping. It's painful to experience the results of poor sowing, but denying God's course corrections blocks us from becoming whole and holy.

• The legitimacy the Exhorter feels must always come from God, not from the need to be needed by other people.

• God uses the pain and suffering caused by our own poor choices to give us course corrections, to grow us up in Him. God is reality. Denying Him comes with a price.

• It's easy for the Exhorter to be irresponsible with time and to refuse to recognize the consequences of poor sowing. He also allows others to cover for him. This is not God's best. God desires the Exhorter to walk in dominion over time and timing to regulate the body of Christ.

• Regulating the body of Christ means the Exhorter comes out of his time of intimacy with the Lord with a clear picture of God's will for the church and His timing on its implementation.

• God's power is never the issue. The power of God is always there, but His character must be revealed to the people, and the Exhorter is the one who takes us there!

Exhorter Blessing

I call the Exhorter portion of your spirit to the front to hear how God sees you and how He made you.

Exhorter, I bless the redeeming power of God in you. You have been made by God to be the greatest light bearer of all the redemptive gifts. The extraordinary light you bring comes from your own intimacy with God, which He uses to draw others into the kingdom of light. This is who you are and who you were made to be in the service of the King.

Exhorter, I bless your desire and skill to communicate God's heart—both to those who know Him and those who have no idea who He is. I bless your ability to cross all barriers (social, economic, racial, religious) to introduce people to God and who He says they are.

Exhorter, I bless you with deep recognition of your birthright, which is based on your design. Who you are and who God made you to be parallels the sun, moon, and stars of the fourth day of creation—the Exhorter's day. You have been made to shed light on God and to communicate Him and His ways to all kinds of people. You are a spiritual (and sometimes physical) globetrotter who never meets a stranger, easily communicating the good news of the gospel of Christ. I bless your unique ability to push through cultural barriers and inspire and mobilize people of all races to advance God's kingdom on earth. When there are differences and conflict, I bless you with bringing harmony and reconciliation so the work of God can move forward.

I bless you, Exhorter, with understanding God's desire for you to develop His wisdom in order to steward the resources He's given you. I bless you to receive the best God has for you by focusing on the vertical first—making your relationship with Him the priority of your life—and then sowing into the horizontal relationships around you. I bless you with this promise, "But seek first his kingdom and his righteousness, and all these things will be given to you as well" (Matthew 6:33). I bless you with mastering the principle of sowing and reaping.

I bless you, Exhorter, with bringing the pure light of the revelation of God out of the time you spend in His presence. I bless you with allowing the Lord to heal the hurts in your spirit, soul, and body so you'll stay true to the light He gives you. As you bring others into His presence, I bless you to resist fears of rejection that may have plagued your ability to be His messenger in the past.

I bless you, Exhorter, as God's magnificent timepiece. You are to know His time and timing for the body of Christ, and I bless you with walking in dominion over time in your own life. I bless you with developing the potential God's placed in you, moving toward excellent control of time as He prepares you for leadership in the days ahead.

I bless you with all these blessings in the mighty name of Jesus Christ.

Chapter 8

The Redemptive Gift of Giver

"EVERY DAY *we are bombarded with a myriad of personality assessments, self-improvement scales, and success programs telling us what we need to do and accomplish in order to reach fulfillment and find purpose in life. As Christian believers we hear over and over that God has a plan and purpose for our lives, but how do we get to that divine plan?*

"Finding out the Giver was my primary redemptive gift has not only provided the clarity I needed for fulfilling the purpose for my being on earth, but is showing me I do not have to find the plan because the plan is in me! It was embedded in my spiritual DNA and decided long before I was born. My task is to allow my spirit to work with the Holy Spirit to unpack the resources Father God has placed within me to be used in my daily walk with Him.

"Receiving the knowledge of the Giver's specific characteristics has provided tremendous understanding of how I am spiritually wired in target areas of strength and needed improvement, as well as how I approach life situations. This has helped me understand myself better, and I am now trying to stop comparing myself so much to others who I believe are more gifted than I am. Just think! God has expressed His tremendous love for me by placing in my spiritual identity the makings of the Giver—nurturer, birther, and protector of new things. I am now free to be the ME God designed me to be!"

— *E. Giles*

Behavioral Characteristics

GENERATIONAL GIFT	reflects God as a family man (like the Teacher and Ruler)
	always looking to "do" family, to create a family environment wherever he goes
BIRTHER	protector
	nurturer of new things
	has a greater ability to reproduce that which will continue for generations to come
VERY FLEXIBLE	very diverse
	the most difficult gift to peg
	able to relate to a wide range of people
	involved in a variety of projects and activities
EXPERIENCES FAVOR	includes all resources, including money
	wise in handling money
	sensitive to being conned or manipulated
"NO LIMITS" INDIVIDUAL	struggles with accepting there are no more options left in a situation
	lives in the present moment
	tends not to learn from the past
	doesn't like to be confronted on issues more than a week old
	can lack a sense of gratitude
NATURAL NETWORKER	brings people together and persuades them to do things
	handles the tension of working with a group of people who don't see eye-to-eye
RELIGIOUS	may do the right thing for the wrong reasons
	tends toward being a religious person rather than a spiritual person

can struggle with faith due to his
failure to invest in knowing God and
learning how to trust Him to provide

The Giver in Scripture

When God creates life He goes all the way. He is an
abundant creator Who does what He does with great diversity,
creativity, and flair. New life requires new birth, and God has
deposited the special anointing to birth, nurture, and protect
new life in the spiritual DNA of the Giver.

God spoke: "Swarm, Ocean, with fish and all sea life!
Birds, fly through the sky over Earth!"
God created the huge whales,
all the swarm of life in the waters,
And every kind and species of flying birds.
God saw that it was good.
God blessed them: "Prosper! Reproduce! Fill Ocean!
Birds, reproduce on Earth!"
It was evening, it was morning—
Day Five.

Genesis 1:20-23

God told Abram: "Leave your country, your family, and your
father's home for a land that I will show you.
I'll make you a great nation
and bless you.
I'll make you famous;
you'll be a blessing.
I'll bless those who bless you;
those who curse you I'll curse.
All the families of the Earth
will be blessed through you."

Genesis 12:1-3

Giver Application

1.   You teem with life! "Teem" means to be abundantly fertile or to bring forth life. The fifth day of creation parallels your magnificent gift: "And God said, 'Let the waters teem with living creatures, and let birds fly above the earth across the vault of the sky'" (Genesis 1:20). You are very versatile, diverse, and productive in your interests.

2.   The life God created on the fifth day was life in the blood—the birds and the fish—so you are concerned with life and everything that comes with it. You possess the spiritual authority to protect new birth. Your prayers can prevent the devouring of a ministry, a program, or whatever the new thing is.

3.   Like the Teacher before you, you are a generational gift. This means that whatever you do, whether good or bad, it is more likely to be carried on by the generations (physical and spiritual seed) that follow.

4.   You are designed and anointed by God to bless. How do we know this? On the Giver's day of creation, God blessed for the very first time that which He had created. Pay attention anytime God mentions something for the first time. In this case, this is where the art of blessing began—on your day, Giver!

5.   You are to give more than money to the world. You are made to release generational blessings into your family line. Abraham was the redemptive gift of Giver. He lived by faith and it was accounted to him as righteousness. Think of the impact of the blessing of faith Abraham passed down to all of us who are children of God!

6.   You have been made by God to be independent, to not need other people, and you may not even acknowledge your needs to God. This can be your downfall. You tend to be casual about holiness, but God requires it.

7.   The missing link for you is oftentimes your relationship with God. God did make you independent, but not from Him.

The Birthright and Battlefield for the Redemptive Gift of Giver

The birthright is to release life-giving generational blessings into the family line and to birth life-giving systems and organizations through holiness and intimacy with God.

I've known many people with the redemptive gift of Giver, but none like the one I've been married to for twenty-plus years. Like most married couples, we have certainly struggled because of the differences between us, but these differences are not so "between" us anymore. We've come to recognize that this hardwiring from God is the real deal, and this knowledge has helped us give more grace to one another. (If that particular quirky characteristic comes from the heart of God, who am I to try and change it?)

As I began to recognize the redemptive gift of Giver in my husband, I began to celebrate the man God had given me. As we both studied the redemptive gifts and their parallels to the seven days of creation, we recognized some amazing things. As long as I'd known Fred (and before), he'd been a fish keeper. Wherever we lived he had to have an aquarium, a pond, or both. In one home he managed to construct and stock a 400-gallon saltwater tank. I absolutely had no grid for this at all. Later, I began to study the different redemptive gifts and how they paralleled creation. Would you believe it was on the fifth day of creation—the Giver's day—that God created everything with which the water teems! Can you spell F-I-S-H? What we had chalked up to one well-developed hobby was actually the deposited DNA of God in Fred that drew him to express this design of teeming life! God had drawn Fred to this very aspect of his creative nature for years and we hadn't even known it!

It is startling, even amazing, to watch the Giver come up with endless ideas and projects. The creativity just pours out of him.

When I came into the understanding of the redemptive gifts and the power God puts into His designs, my relationship with Fred began to make sense. He cannot *not* create, and why should he? He is a builder by profession, so the gift is amplified. As my gifts (Mercy and Prophet) drew me to become a professional counselor, Fred's gifts drew him to be a builder. It is a part of who God made him to be—a creator. It would be foolish to think Fred was responsible for that career path alone.

In the beginning I was startled, even irritated by my husband's seemingly endless energy for new ideas and projects. At one point (regrettably) I snapped, "Your thoughts freak me out!" Obviously, this did not help our marriage much. Differences in energy levels were also a point of contention, as the Mercy is a slow mover and the Giver needs little sleep. I still laugh when I think about him saying that he wished he didn't have to sleep so he could get more done. No sleep! Are you kidding?

As often happens, our understanding of God's hand in all this came a bit later. It seems easy to recognize now the blending of our gifts—Giver and Mercy. We became involved in the ministries of Celebrate Recovery and Love in the Name of Christ in our community. The former ministers to people who struggle with addictions; the latter aims to transform lives in the name of Christ. In both, Fred was pivotal in beginning and establishing the foundations of the programs, and I was a foot soldier who provided one-on-one counseling support and ministry.

I once heard an interesting concept. God puts men and women together in marriage for more than just the obvious reasons. They marry because they are attracted to one another, want to have a family, and want the security marriage brings; but they are also brought together to be a fortress for the kingdom of God.

This was one of those statements I believe the Holy Spirit made to my spirit many years ago. I was searching for meaning, a deeper meaning to this portion of my life. I did not know about the human spirit or the redemptive gifts of God. Now I understand the combination of gifts God gives a man and wife can, when working together in unity, accomplish great things when serving His purposes. This is something the spirit thrills to. Eternal purposes that go well beyond the good things of earth ... can you hear that with your spirit? You should.

The battlefield for the Giver is whether he will have a stewardship or an ownership mindset. In truth, we receive everything from God. The Giver, however, can become fearful and controlling, using resources for himself or holding onto resources for fear of losing them. This is an ownership mindset, which is not God's best. The better, higher way is to be God's steward, receiving resources from Him and partnering with Him fulfill His agenda. God wants to give us the blessings He gave Abraham, but this will only come out of a relationship of holiness and intimacy with Him

• Integrity, relationship, and faith will flow when the Giver is submitted to God and puts his relationship with God before all others.

• The battle is to allow God to make him safe and secure and not rely on his own ability to do things. "God can do absolutely nothing with a man who will not admit that he needs anything from God" (*If I Perish, I Perish*, 1967, 20).

• The principle of stewardship is the key law of truth that applies to the Giver. It is what God calls the Giver to walk in. And since most Givers can make things happen, an ownership mindset is easy to fall into.

• The mind of faith knows it all belongs to God. He is in control. This frees us—everything begins and ends with God, and we can't take it with us when we go!

• Givers do well to remember that leaving a spiritual inheritance is more important than leaving physical assets behind—one of knowing God, His Word, and His promises.

Giver Blessing

Beloved, I call the Giver portion of your spirit to the front in the name of Jesus Christ of Nazareth.

Giver, I want to celebrate the gift of life God has deposited in you. You parallel the fifth day of creation, a day of great diversity and multiplication. Recognize this truth with your spirit as you hear the Word of God for you: "And God said, 'Let the water teem with living creatures, and let birds fly above the earth across the vault of the sky.' So God created the great creatures of the sea and every living thing and moving thing with which the water teems according to their kinds, and every winged bird according to its kind. And God saw that it was good. God blessed them and said, 'Be fruitful and increase in number and fill the waters in the seas, and let the birds increase on the earth.' And there was evening and there was morning—the fifth day" (Genesis 1:20-23).

Giver, I bless your immense creativity and obedience to partner with God to allow Him to bring forth life-giving systems and organizations through you.

Giver, you have been made by God to birth, nurture, and protect new life. You reflect that aspect of God, the family man, because you were made to create family wherever you go. I bless you, Giver, for your generational worldview—your deep desire to prepare the way for your family and others who will follow after you.

Giver, I bless your extreme diversity and adaptability. You are a "no limits" kind of person who is involved in many things. You are made to teem with life. I bless this life to come as a result of faith in God, not reliance on your own skillset.

I bless you, Giver, to walk in great faith in a culture that rejects dependence on God. I bless you to identify with the biblical example of your redemptive gift—Job. Many misunderstand the message in the story of Job, who walked with the keenest awareness he was a steward of the blessings God had given him. He understood that he owned nothing and God owned everything, including his life. Job trusted that God knew what He was doing, that Job's life was in God's hands, and that God owned Job's life, not the other way around.

So I bless you, Giver, with great faith for overcoming your tendency to fear and take control. If you choose to believe these lies, the result will be the undesirable fruits of arrogance and fear in your life. I bless you to recognize the potential God's given you to release His life to those around you. I bless you with making peace with God and allowing Him to direct you in the work He has given you to do. I bless you with increasing peace as you operate in the fear of the Lord, which "leads to life; then one rests content, untouched by trouble (Proverbs 19:23).

I bless you, Giver, with imparting life-giving, generational blessings to your physical and spiritual seed as you do the work God has called you to do—for His kingdom to come upon the earth as it is in heaven. I bless you in Jesus' mighty name.

Chapter 9

The Redemptive Gift of Ruler

"UNDERSTANDING I *am a Ruler shows me it's easy for me to be more task oriented than people oriented. I try to stay aware of that and to be more intentional. I constantly bring my mind back to ask the question: "Is this what God wants even though I know I have the ability to do this? Does He want me to insert myself into this? Does He want me to lead or just be a team member?" God's given me some amazing abilities that really shine, but they can shine even in my own strength. This is a stronghold I must be aware of—doing things in my own power. Freedom comes when I remain in the will of God."*

—J. Rodriguez

"UNDERSTANDING MY *redemptive gifts of Prophet and Ruler has given me a greater depth of knowledge of myself and the role I play in the world. I believe it has freed me to be more of who I am and what I was meant to be. Before I understood this I held back, trying to lie low and not be such a big voice in the room. Now I am more comfortable than ever with my leadership, my ability to see things others do not understand, and my ability to lead people down a trail—even when most of the time there is no trail there. I now understand I have a pioneering spirit in these gifts that calls me to lead others into new places with new life-giving ideas and divine design. That has helped me in my business and my mission as well."*

— D. Farah

Behavioral Characteristics

SPIRITUAL FATHER	made to nurture the human spirit (like the Teacher and Giver)
GOD'S EMPIRE BUILDER	made by God to look at anything and want to make it bigger (like Noah, Solomon, Nehemiah, Joseph)
	takes a vision, breaks it down, and puts an effective plan together to implement
CLEAR LEADER	thrives under pressure
	likes to put others under pressure
	is in excellent control of his time
	gets the job done
RESILIENT	can withstand strong opposition
	takes on more tasks than is normally possible in order to finish in the time allowed
	has tremendous ability to focus
OWNS HIS PROBLEMS	doesn't look to other people for help
	has no welfare mentality whatsoever
	give him the job, the deadline, and the resources and get out of his way!
INDEPENDENT	but not malicious
	although he may not need others, others need him
STRATEGIC	knows how to position imperfect people in organizations
	brings out the best in people

The Ruler in Scripture

Unprecedented life came on the sixth day of creation, the Ruler's day. This was the day God created animals, insects, and human beings. God's blessing on the Ruler is to prosper, reproduce, fill the earth, and subdue it

God spoke: "Earth, generate life! Every sort and kind:

cattle and reptiles and wild animals—all kinds."
And there it was:
    wild animals of every kind,
Cattle of all kinds, every sort of reptile and bug.
    God saw that it was good.
God spoke: "Let us make human beings in our image, make them
    reflecting our nature
So they can be responsible for the fish in the sea,
    the birds in the air, the cattle,
And, yes, Earth itself,
    and every animal that moves on the face of Earth."
God created human beings;
    he created them godlike,
Reflecting God's nature.
    He created them male and female.
God blessed them:
    "Prosper! Reproduce! Fill Earth! Take charge!
Be responsible for fish in the sea and birds in the air,
    for every living thing that moves on the face of Earth."
Then God said, "I've given you
    every sort of seed-bearing plant on Earth
And every kind of fruit-bearing tree,
    given them to you for food.
To all animals and all birds,
    everything that moves and breathes,
I give whatever grows out of the ground for food."
    And there it was.
God looked over everything he had made;
    it was so good, so very good!
It was evening, it was morning—Day Six.

Genesis 1:24-31

Ruler Application

1.   On the sixth day of creation (the Ruler's day) God breathed life into the first man, creating the human spirit. So as good as you are at organizing and leading people, God's primary purpose for the Ruler is to nurture people's spirits. In this way, the community you develop is based on unity of spirit, not just getting a task done.

2.   True leadership is not about titles or positions, but is based on the degree to which you are submitted to God's law and are life-giving to those around you.

You develop spiritual authority when you do three things:

—receive from God,

—give others what God's given you, and

—walk in dominion.

This is the sequence for the Ruler as well as all the gifts.

3.   The word dominion can be a bit intimidating, but there's no mystery here—it is simply partnering with God to do His will in His time.

4.   Dominion is the gift God gave very specifically to the Ruler on the sixth day of creation—when He told Adam to both subdue the earth and have dominion over every living creature (Genesis 1:28).

5.   You possess a special authority to bless. Why? Because God blessed and gave dominion to man on the Ruler's day. You have an authority in blessing that passes on authority to other people. Some people can bless you and it's nice, but in a few hours or a few days it's gone and forgotten. But there are other people who know who they are in God and possess their birthrights as nurturers to the spirit. The blessing they speak to you imparts spiritual power and authority to you. You don't forget it and you are never the same again.

6.   You can be tempted to exert power to get the job done, but God shows you how true power is found in His love!

The Birthright and Battlefield for the Redemptive Gift of Ruler

The birthright—who the Ruler is and who he is meant to be—is a person who imparts authority by blessing his physical and spiritual seed.

Physical seed refers to your natural born children. Spiritual seed refers to those you mentor who are in a spiritual relationship with you.

I have no children of my own, so it has been a tremendous reward to be a spiritual parent to others. In His lovingkindness, God has compensated me in this way. I consider the spiritual coaching I do a reflection of the Ruler portion of God's nature in me. This is because the Ruler is made to nurture people's spirits.

Another part of the birthright of the redemptive gift of Ruler is to go beyond obeying God to honoring Him. This means to seek God's desires above your own and to lead a lifestyle of freedom and holiness by placing the entire contents of your life in God's hands.

The battlefield is freedom vs. slavery. Freedom for the Ruler comes down to a desire to depend on and honor the Lord more than build the Ruler's own kingdom. Rulers are so very gifted to get things done and to get people to do things, so it's easy for them to believe they must rely on themselves instead of God. This is the lie Satan has been trying to get us all to buy since the Garden of Eden. It is a trap for us all, but even more so for the Ruler. Rulers are made by God to be excellent in completing tasks, but God never meant for the task to get ahead of His power demonstrated in love and truth.

God's power source is love.

This section would not be complete without including the story of one of God's great Rulers, a man by the name of Gunnar Olson. In May 2003 I had the amazing privilege of spending one afternoon sitting in Gunnar Olson's living room, watching and listening while this man shared from his heart about the Lord. The fullness of God was so great in this man that I began to weep (and couldn't stop for quite some time before leaving his home).

In 1985, this Swedish plastics manufacturer founded the International Christian Chamber of Commerce (ICCC), an international organization whose mission it is to bring God's kingdom rule to the marketplaces of the world through its local and national chambers. ICCC was born out of Gunnar's heart to go beyond being a mere Christian businessman to being a vessel—one the Lord could use in the marketplace to bring the breath and life of God to people and nations.

In his book *Business Unlimited, Memories of the Coming Kingdom* (2004), Gunnar tells the story of how the Lord gave him great favor with people, businessmen, and even heads of state as he came and brought God's power for healing and restoration to their situations. The thing that distinguishes this man from many others is his decisive dedication to honoring the Lord and his recognition (from God) that love is the key to our lives, not power. Gunnar learned that when you break the law of love, the consequence is the disappearance of the presence of God. Time and time again the Lord showed Gunnar the way to love people and things, and as Gunnar followed God's promptings (often to the agony of his soul), miracles happened.

Jesus said, "Truly I tell you, if anyone says to this mountain, 'Go, throw yourself into the sea,' and does not doubt in their heart but believes that what they say will happen, it will be done for them" (Mark 11:23). The Ruler is called to have dominion over created things. Gunnar dared to believe the Word of God and by faith spoke to "mountains" to move, and they did. His spirit was alive and attentive to the Spirit of God in such a way that he forgot himself and just did what God wanted him to do, which resulted in God getting great glory!

Many businessmen and women believe the only legitimate

way to serve the Lord is behind a pulpit, but God showed Gunnar how to bring the kingdom of God right down to the factory floor—to the marketplace itself.

This study of the redemptive gifts is one tool God's using to position us to be able to redeem our entire culture, the majority of which exists outside the four walls of the church!

Rulers must study ways to do the things they are already called to do and discover (with the help of the Holy Spirit) the particular way that will bring honor and glory to God! This calls for humility in the Ruler, which is greatly pleasing to God.

The birthright is not to make a slave of yourself and everyone around you by getting a tremendous amount of work done, but to earn spiritual authority by being obedient and honoring God. Then the Ruler will have dominion over spiritual things and be able to release that dominion to the generations that follow. The foundation must be a bedrock of righteousness. This is the seedbed for everything that God wants to release through the redemptive gift of Ruler.

Ruler Blessing

Beloved, I call the Ruler portion of your spirit to the front. Ruler, you parallel the sixth day of creation—the day God created animals, insects, and human beings. Here is a vivid picture of your tremendous design. The DNA of God inside you reflects the ever expanding nature of God, His universe, and the wide diversity found in His creation.

I bless you, Ruler, with knowing in your spirit that you are made in the image of God. I bless you with deep recognition that you are a son to your Father, and the gifts He's deposited in you are good. Not only did God create you in His very own image (Genesis 1:27), but He commanded you to be fruitful, multiply, fill the earth, and subdue it (Genesis 1:28).

I bless you, Ruler, to receive God's breath of life inside you. Breath represents spirit—your innermost being, the part of you made to receive directly from God. The Word of God in Genesis 2:7 states, "The Lord God formed the man from the dust of the ground and breathed into his nostrils the breath of life, and the man became a living being." God is spirit and He nurtures your spirit. I bless you with allowing the Lord to nurture you so you can nurture the spirit of those He brings into your life.

I bless you, Ruler, with winning the battle of freedom versus slavery. You may have been trained or conditioned as a child by an authority figure who did not know his God. Consequently, the slave master (Satan) may have established a beachhead in your life. I bless your spirit with hearing the Spirit of Truth speak and tell you who you are in God's eyes, and that your legitimacy is in Him and Him alone. Make no mistake: your great ability to motivate and lead—to take a vision, break it down, and put together an effective plan—is your redemptive gift from God. I bless you to remain submitted to God's agenda as you do the work He has planned in advance for you to do: the work of life-giving leadership that frees.

I bless you, Ruler, to know your birthright in full, not just the part that may come easily to you. I bless you to blend the great anointing of God to work with people and get things done, with an equal anointing to nurture people's spirits in the values of the everlasting kingdom of our God and His Christ.

In Jesus' mighty name, I bless you.

Chapter 10

The Redemptive Gift of Mercy

"I AM *a grandmother who has a seven-month-old grandson I care for several days a week. I began blessing my grandson's spirit at the age of five months. I would lay him on his back, put one hand on his stomach, and read a blessing from* Pure Joy *(book by Arthur Burk and Crystal Wade).*

"From day one, my grandson absolutely loved the pink cover (of the book). He would smile and flail his arms up and down as I called his spirit to attention and blessed him. Eye contact was not a problem. He would look me in the eyes and smile this huge smile that melted my heart.

"Day after day, I began to notice that whenever I pulled out the "pink" book, he would immediately flail his arms and be captivated. I also noticed I had become very committed to blessing him every day. Over this period of time, there were a couple of days that, due to schedule changes and activities, I would get home and realize I had not blessed him that day. My heart sank within me to the point that it ached over the opportunity I had missed. I didn't realize how committed I had become to nurturing his spirit (and mine) through these daily blessings.

"I do not leave his home now without blessing him, no matter what. At seven months, when I call his spirit to attention, my grandson looks at me with those big brown eyes as if he's saying, "Bring it on, I'm ready!"

— *R. Allen*

Behavioral Characteristics

CROWN JEWEL — worshipper; worships God

harmonizes all the gifts — fills up with God's presence, then leads others into God's presence at a deep and intimate level

"BE" NOT "DO" — "feels" life, doesn't just "do" life like others

moves slowly and adapts to change slowly

exacts the deepest amount of insight, wisdom, and understanding from what's going on around him

HIGHLY SENSITIVE — sensitive to the spiritual atmosphere and to others

deep reactions to common hurts —

a popular person

will usually have only a few close friends with whom he shares everything

"triggered"

allergic to confrontation of any kind

will please others to gain their approval

"victim" spirit — not nurtured in spirit .

craves emotional intimacy and physical touch

wants to be physically close

MINISTER TO THE HURT — speaks the language of love

is a very safe person with whom others can share their pain

Slower to process

absorbs pain and tension around him so he can become a burden bearer for others

spirit of grief.

is famous for taking up an offense on behalf of a third party

SOFT AND STUBBORN — very sensitive

weak reconciliation skill

once deeply hurt, can shut down any chance of returning to intimacy with the one who has offended him

TUNED TO ALIGNMENT — knows when relationships and things are correctly aligned

allergic to confrontation

— 96 —

Stubborn . Comes out of unforgiveness.

Pride in denial .—

[handwritten margin notes: "mercy heart", "Knows - intuitive", "of God", "mind of God — Prophet.", "increase — of God's", "decrease what saying"]

can recognize both when things are out
of order and when order is harmonious
and life-giving

celebrates when things are good, right,
and true

HEARS GOD'S HEART — knows and follows the heart of God at a
deep level

The Mercy in Scripture

Understand that holiness is central to the redemptive gift of
Mercy. For the first time, and on the seventh day of creation
(the day that parallels this gift), God blessed time and made it
holy.

[handwritten margin note: "Bless time"]

Heaven and Earth were finished,
  down to the last detail.
By the seventh day

God had finished his work.
On the seventh day

he rested from all his work.
God blessed the seventh day.

He made it a Holy Day
Because on that day he rested from his work,
  all the creating God had done.
This is the story of how it all started,
  of Heaven and Earth when they were created.

Genesis 2:1-4:

"Now make a lid of pure gold for the Chest,
  an Atonement-Cover,
three and three-quarters feet long
  and two and one-quarter feet wide.

[handwritten margin note: "1 Tim 1:7"]

"Sculpt two winged angels out of hammered gold
  for either end of the Atonement-Cover,
one angel at one end, one angel at the other.

Make them of one piece with the Atonement-Cover.
Make the angels with their wings spread,
     hovering over the Atonement-Cover,
facing one another but looking down on it.
     Set the Atonement-Cover as a lid over the
Chest and place in the Chest
     The Testimony that I will give you.
I will meet you there at set times
     and speak with you from above the Atonement-Cover
and from between the angel-figures that are on it,
     speaking the commands that I have for the Israelites."

Exodus 25:17-22

The mercy seat (as this is called) is the seventh piece of furniture God designated for worship in the tabernacle, and it is a picture of the intimate relationship God desires with the redemptive gift of Mercy.

Mercy Application

The Mercy parallels the seventh day of creation, on which God rested and blessed time (Genesis 2:2-3). God sanctified time for the first time by blessing the day. The Mercy is made by God to sanctify time by blessing it.

1.   You do not fit easily into one category. If this is your primary gift, you should know and accept the fact you think and feel differently to other people.

2.   A crucial value for you is to worship in every part of your life and to live in God's presence. As you do this, you position yourself to receive from God and give to others what God's given to you.

3.   As you worship God in your daily life, you walk in the blessing of the presence of the Lord, which brings cleansing and alignment to corrupted, polluted situations and people.

4.   Many Mercys are broken, wounded people who never

learned what true love is in their childhood years. As a result, you may sacrifice inappropriately (not just to others but also to God) in an effort to keep the peace, stay safe, and avoid conflict.

5.   You are made to "feel" life, not just do it. For this reason you can become a slave to your own appetites and lusts rather than walk in freedom in God. The freedom God gives brings with it responsibility to solve problems. Only when you accept responsibility for the problems God is giving you will you experience true fulfillment.

6.   Your primary issue is to learn to love God and solve the particular problems God's designed you to solve. Your problems will look different from the problems God gives to other gifts because of the way He made you—to "be" rather than "do."

7.   Getting wounded through no fault of your own, not knowing how to love—oftentimes you cannot conceive how God will repay you for wrongs you have suffered. Many times fearful and impatient, you might refuse to wait to receive the gifts of God, taking your life into your own hands (see redemptive gift of Prophet). But God is God and He compensates in His good time. God's compensation is something you must learn to wait for, recognizing that in some cases, the compensation may not come to you but to a future generation.

The Birthright and the Battlefield for the Redemptive Gift of Mercy

There are really two identities in the birthright of every gift: The "who you are"' and the "who God made you to be." God made the Mercy the harmonizer, the synchronizer of the entire body of Christ. For this reason, it is critical for Mercys to get emotional and spiritual healing so they can take their place in the symphony of the human spirit, being the one God has ordained to bring all the other gifts into alignment and harmony with His will.

God wants the Mercy to remain in His presence at all times.

God wants the Mercy to be in constant and continual worship of Him. God wants the Mercy to stand firm on the virtues of the kingdom of God—righteousness, peace, and joy—and exercise dominion over sin and unholy things around him. God wants the Mercy to carry and release the glory and holiness of God in the earth.

This is the Mercy's birthright. This is who the redemptive gift of Mercy is and who God made him to be. It seems the greatest assault that can come against God's design comes against this gift because of the beauty, nobility, and holiness of God Mercy is called to walk in.

The battle is for the full release of the anointing of God in the life of the redemptive gift of Mercy.

Remember, Mercys are made to know love at a deep and intimate level. Out of that deep relationship with God, they are called to love others as they have been loved. However, many Mercys suffer from the effects of some type of abuse, and almost all suffer from spiritual neglect.

In families where there is little emotional, physical, or spiritual nurture, Mercys are particularly vulnerable. The enemy knows that. He takes advantage of this opportunity to derail God's plan, separating the Mercy from God's presence and getting him to focus his attention on relieving his pain.

As a result, the Mercy can become a slave to his own feelings. This plays out in many ways in his life. A mindset impregnated with hopelessness (also known as a stronghold) can attach itself to a Mercy at an early age. This is almost always because he has been mistreated in some way. Without an understanding of who God is and how much God loves him, the Mercy finds it easy to see his identity and legitimacy through the lens of his circumstances instead of God's Word. In my life, there was no understanding that the Word of God was alive, that it spoke to who I was and who God made me to be. This set me up for deep pain in my spirit and soul—pain the enemy fed on for many years.

The deeply sensitive nature of the redemptive gift of Mercy is both an asset and a liability if the Mercy is not firmly attached to the Vine. He needs to receive his strongest sense of belonging, competence, and worth from who God says he is, not from what others need him to be.

True fulfillment will come as the Mercy allows the Spirit of God to heal his spirit. In order to receive this healing, the Mercy must set his heart to be still in God's presence, allow the pain to be healed, and worship God in the splendor of His holiness.

This is the battle: to trade self-gratification for God-gratification, which is the ultimate fulfillment. He must receive first from God and then minister to others from a place of peace, rest, and wholeness.

Mercy Blessing

Beloved, I call the Mercy portion of your spirit to the front to hear how God sees you and how He made you.

The seventh day of creation parallels the redemptive gift of Mercy. This was the day God rested and blessed. Mercy, I bless you with the rest and blessing that comes from time spent in the presence of the Lord. You are the part of God's heart that is most comfortable "being," not "doing," and this reflects the nature of God on the seventh day.

Although you do many things well, your simple desire to be in God's presence is your redemptive gift. It is your spiritual identity, and I bless you to embrace it. I bless you to press into your gift, filling up with His presence so that you bring His tangible presence to those you meet and minister to. God made you to know His heart. I bless you with confidence in knowing what pleases Him most.

I bless you, Mercy, with an increasing understanding of who

you are and who God made you to be, and to understand your birthright. You are to have an intimate, confidential relationship with God, and I bless that. You are made to carry the presence of God. I bless you with bringing the fullness you receive from time spent in His presence to those in the world around you. I bless you to protect the sanctuary of your time, blessing it as God has designed you to do. The time you spend alone with the Lord is preparation for future assignments He has for you that will advance His kingdom.

You are made to walk in great integrity, dignity, and honor as the crown jewel of God's creation. I bless how you walk with a spirit of elegance and beauty. You are made to release the perfume of heaven through your life. You play such a crucial role in maintaining the wellbeing of the human spirit because you know when things are harmonious and when they are not. God has made you to bring the harmony and alignment that is missing in so much of our world today. As you do this, you bring your unique expression of God's nature to others. I bless the revelation you bring, which is nothing less than exquisite. No other gift comes close to expressing God the way you do.

You have been made by God to know His shalom peace in a deeper, more intimate and fulfilling way than any other gift. I bless how easily you enter into the presence of God—to receive from Him—and then bring the blessing of His peace to those around you. I bless you in the name of the Prince of Peace. I bless you in Jesus' name.

Chapter 11

The Ultimate "App"—Your Call in God

As you can see, knowing your redemptive gift is very important. Why? It is your spiritual identity. It is your hardwiring from God, your "bent," and goes a long way toward explaining why you think and feel the way you do.

When you are living in the freedom and fulfillment of God's design of you, you can't get enough of what He's made you to do.

You may recognize, however, that you have been trying to be someone you're not and were never meant to be. You couldn't be sure of God's opinion on the subject and had no trust in your own judgment either. Perhaps you've been trying to be like others, feeling "less than," resentful, and even hopeless as a result.

God does not expect you to figure everybody else out. He's ready for you to nail down who you are in Him first. Then you can take the insights you've gained and use them to minister to other people. Understanding yourself will help you to understand others more easily.

First Commandment First

"The most important one," answered Jesus, "is this: 'Hear, O Israel: The Lord our God, the Lord is one. Love the Lord your God with all your heart and with all your soul and with all your mind and with all your strength.' The second is this: 'Love your neighbor as yourself.' There is no commandment greater than these" (Mark 12:29-31).

God wants us to receive His love so we can obey His first commandment first. The Spirit of God wants to minister to your spirit about who you are, how He sees you, and what He has made you to do. Then, from the wellspring of love (He is love) inside you, you will worship Him by loving your neighbor as yourself. It's like we haven't trusted ourselves or God enough to just be with Him and let Him show us His way. When we are flowing spirit to spirit with the living God, our lives are a living testimony to His goodness, kindness, and strength. So many Christians (as well as other people) are weary because they have never followed God's sequence for their lives. The abundant life He died to give us bursts open when we receive our greatest sense of belonging, competence, and worth from Him. From that place of great legitimacy, we move out to bless others.

God expects us to receive everything that comes from Him first, not give Him something first. He is love, He is truth, He is the way. Until we get this on the inside—deep inside—we won't feel fully legitimate in Him and we'll go nowhere. God makes this very clear: "Every good and perfect gift is from above, coming down from the Father of the heavenly lights, who does not change like shifting shadows" (James 1:17). One way God wants to show you who He is, is by showing you who you are. He made us in His image and we are a reflection of His grace and beauty. When you begin to see this and know you are good in His eyes, you will love Him with everything in you. Wait a minute ... isn't that the first commandment?

And then you will be in a position to love your neighbor as yourself.

So many Christians and folk in general are close to burnout from putting the second commandment first. They are blind to the fact that God is passionate to give them all the identity and legitimacy they could ever hope for in Him!

We've gotten all hung up because we cannot truly give to another, even to God, until we have received His love in our spirits (in that unique and beautiful way we were made to do). Once we do, we are in a position to love Him back with all that is in us.

The passion God has deposited in you will never die. Why? Because it is of Him, and this makes it eternal. So even if you have never felt you could do the things God says you can do, the nurturing of your spirit with the truth of how God made you will enable you to grow right where you are.

There is no deeper, more fundamental identity than this—the part of God's eternal nature in you, your spiritual DNA—your redemptive gift.

We each receive God's love in our own way, based on the different ways He's made us. Learning our identity helps us receive God's love in the particular way He designed us to receive it.

In the movie *Chariots of Fire*, the true story of England's quest to win the 1924 Olympic Games, runner Eric Liddell spoke of how he could feel God's pleasure when he ran. This is a vivid example of how God designs each of us for fulfillment in Him. When Liddell was doing the thing God designed him to do, he not only felt God's pleasure, but it also brought glory to God. The same is true for us when we activate our redemptive gifts.

The Prophet feels God's pleasure when he provides vision to others to live according to God's plan.

The Servant feels God's pleasure when he gives support to others, especially leaders.

The Teacher feels the pleasure of God in finding truth and

making sure others know what it is.

The Exhorter feels the exhilaration of God while he crosses every barrier to tell people who God is.

The Giver experiences the teeming life of God in a never-ending pursuit of new ideas and inventions.

The Ruler feels God's pleasure while he is propelled to expand the kingdom of God.

The Mercy is most alive in the presence of God and takes His presence with him wherever he goes!

This really brings new meaning to, "For it is God who works in you to will and to act in order to fulfill his good purpose" (Philippians 2:13), doesn't it? Hallelujah!

∽

Let's Be Honest

There are times I must fight to keep hold of my identity and legitimacy, and if you're honest, you do too.

We have to fight, because we have an enemy who does not want us to walk through this life in peace, power, and the presence of the Lord. Nevertheless, God has ordained that we should live in the now, a time that is no time for sissies. "For the Spirit God gave us does not make us timid, but gives us power, love and self-discipline" (II Timothy 1:7), and God wants to manifest His glory through big-spirited sons and daughters like you and me. He wants to reflect His glory to a world that does not know Him. "His intent was that now, through the church, the manifold wisdom of God should be made known to the rulers and authorities in the heavenly realms" (Ephesians 3:10).

∽

In your family, you should have received your strongest sense of identity and legitimacy from your father. Your father should give you your name and tell you what your family stands for. Your father should introduce you to God. This is the love you should receive from your father, yet it is rarely the case. Most of us have grown up with no strong sense of identity, and we allow our more superficial nature (the soul) to tell us if we're legitimate or not. This should not be. If we will receive our heavenly Father's love in our spirits, we will be rooted and grounded for life, and no man and no demon will be able to shake us from what we know the truth to be.

When I was growing up, one of my greatest memories was of my dad saying to me, "Dorinda Davis, the people's choice!" I didn't even know what it meant, but I knew how it made me feel—fantastic! I felt I was important and smart, and I could do anything. This is the stuff of legitimacy, yet it wasn't enough when, years later, I could make no sense of my life and felt I should end it.

I had received my dad's love but never received the love of God my Father in my spirit. I know now I am a redemptive gift of Prophet. The Prophet has a strong need to make sense of everything. It made no sense to me that I could do all I had done and still feel so adrift on the sea of life. I had relied on my own judgment to solve my problems and worked very hard to do lots of things to prove myself "legit." What I now know is:

The love of God is the only true source of legitimacy.

With the love of God under your belt, you are now positioned to do what He has made you to do. Listen with your spirit to the Word of God for you: "For we are God's handiwork, created in Christ Jesus to do good works, which God prepared in advance for us to do" (Ephesians 2:10). These good works are your call or assignment from God. As you can see, each gift demonstrates a particular ability, empowerment, or authority from God. Some would say it is the anointing of God.

When, by faith, you operate according to God's design and exercise your ability or authority in God (allowing Him to lead and guide you in it), good things will happen.

People will get set free as you tell them how God designed them (Prophet).

Leaders will get the support they need to stay strong as leaders (Servant).

Families will be strengthened and unified by learning who God is in real life (Teacher).

People from all races and backgrounds will come together to do God's will (Exhorter).

Family environments will be created to pass blessings on to the next generation (Giver).

God's work will be significantly expanded (Ruler).

Wounded people will be ministered to and healed (Mercy).

These are but a few of the assignments or calls we have before God, based on our design in Him. God will get much more specific with each one of us. What is He whispering to you?

~

A Cultural Pattern Emerges

It's important to note that most children in our culture go the way I went. It is practically impossible for a child to recognize his true (spiritual) identity and feel a sense of legitimacy (know he is right with God). It's even more difficult to understand why God made him and what his purpose is in God if his spirit isn't nurtured. Nurture helps him to know who he is and what God made him to do, which is his birthright. Unless that child receives nurturing in the deepest part of his being (his spirit, the part that witnesses to the truth), the child can very quickly become like a ship on the sea, tossed and turned by the waves of life's circumstances.

When there are no big-spirited adults around to recognize and nurture a child's spirit, the results can be disastrous. I was a perfect example of this—so tender and so intense (Mercy and Prophet) as a child, I took everything to heart. Things said and done hurt me deeply, and no one knew how to deal with me or help me through the pain.

The enemy likes to take those damaged emotions from childhood and feed us on them for a lifetime, keeping us in bondage and cycles of more and more pain. The results include, but are not limited to: a broken identity—sexual and otherwise; a sense of personal isolation; a fear of standing up for oneself; a mistrust of one's own perceptions; and alienation from others and from God.

> *Make No Mistake: The power of a unique and intimate connection between your spirit and the spirit of the living God cannot be underestimated.*

We are living in a time of great shifting as our culture becomes more and more hostile to the gospel of Jesus Christ, to the Truth. It's not just the name of Jesus that provokes the outcry, but who He is—absolute truth, and wherever truth is being attacked, He is under siege. Thus we, as believers, are under siege.

To walk through this time in the strength and peace God intends for us, we must know who we are and what He has made us to do. We must get our legitimacy from Him and Him alone, and not from one another. We must determine to invest in the nurture and development of our spirits and our children's spirits, so we can grow big and strong in Him and move out into the purposes for which He has made us. We will be fulfilled, because in doing so we will be fulfilling Him.

I've made these points at the end to motivate you to become fiercely intentional about nurturing your spirit. There is no mystery here. Your spirit is malnourished. Your spirit is hungry and thirsty. At best, your spirit is suffering from benign neglect and at worst, from outright abuse. Your spirit needs acknowledgment and affirmation. Simply acknowledging your spirit can have a powerful effect on you. God is ready to meet you where you are. (One way to nurture your spirit is to simply read aloud the blessing to your spirit in the first chapter of this book.)

I don't think I'd still have your attention if you were not seeking more, the "much more" of who you are and who you are made to be. Believer or not, identity and legitimacy is the domain of God. The truth is He really did make you according to His purpose, and it is His design of you, and your choice to daily live according to it, that will bring you the greatest sense of fulfillment in your life.

I bless you with being drawn to salvation in Jesus by receiving His love deep in your spirit. And for those who already know Him, I bless you with increasing joy and intimacy as you allow your spirit to receive His richest blessings. I bless the beautiful gift you are in the name of Jesus Christ, Who is the most precious gift of all. I bless you!

Chapter 12

A Developed Spirit

"I **FIRST** *became aware of the idea of nurturing the human spirit about five years ago. A friend gave me a book with blessings I could read aloud to a person. The idea was that the person's spirit could receive information and healing even if the person's soul (mind, will, and emotions) could not understand the blessings. As a person's spirit was nurtured, his spirit could grow bigger and stronger. In fact the spirit could get larger than the soul and take dominion over the soul realm. This was an extremely intriguing idea that really stirred my own spirit. I felt led to begin reading the blessings aloud over some of my most fragile wounded clients.*

"*One person in particular had a vibrant faith in God but continued to struggle with emotional instability resulting from years of abuse. I began reading blessings over her in our therapy sessions. The client reported great gains between sessions. She couldn't wait to come to her next appointment to hear more! This person lived alone and did not have anyone in her life who could read the blessings over her day to day.*

"*I stumbled on the idea of recording the blessings on a small digital recorder. I would read the blessing with her name inserted in it. I recorded various ones over the course of about six months. The client reported to me that having these recordings to listen to helped her stay grounded and stable. She listened to the blessings so much, often having the recording going over and over while she slept, that over time she could speak out long passages of the blessings to herself.*

"Over time, my work with this client took a different path and I forgot she had the recordings. She had a brother who struggled with MS who was getting progressively worse—in and out of the hospital and near death many times. He cursed God and let everyone know he wanted to die. He lapsed into a coma during one lengthy hospitalization. My client recalled the power of the blessings in her own life, so she took the recordings and began playing them in her brother's hospital room. She wasn't certain if they would have any impact since her brother was in a coma. She continued this for about six weeks.

"When her brother came out of the coma, she noticed he was calmer and even a bit receptive to the recordings. He continued to struggle with intense pain, and his legs were twisted into such painful contortions that he was unable to be out of bed. He could not even sit in a wheelchair. Day after day, a team of physical therapists tried to straighten his legs, but as soon as the sessions were over, his legs would revert back to their contorted positions. My client continued to play the recorded blessings and noticed her brother was increasingly receptive to them.

"One day, as the blessings were playing in her brother's hospital room, she witnessed his legs relaxing into a straight position with no more contortions. Everyone was shocked and amazed, especially her brother. The next day, the nurses had her brother sitting up in a wheelchair! He was telling people God had healed him and he was going to be able to go home. This was the very first time my client had ever heard her brother do anything but curse God. Since that time, her brother has continued to improve. He was released from the hospital and is now living at his home. He tells people God healed him!"

— *Susan Goertz*

THE LORD is speaking to all of us.

Listen with your spirit to the revealed word of God to you:

Look around you now. The mercy of God is all around. There is light and beauty in the faces of the people surrounding you.

This is the heavenly realm. I came down to open your eyes to the heavenly realm around you. There is also a hellish realm that is at work. I want to open the eyes of your understanding to be able to see them both and to be able to walk in all the authority and dominion you were originally intended to walk in—the way I did when I walked on the earth.

The enemy has done much to interfere with My plan, but he will not be successful, for I am turning your attention to the thing that counts the most—your spirit in Me. It is time for you to understand that I have many things to give you, and it is safe for you to trust Me to give you the wisdom and understanding you need to live abundantly in this earth. You have everything you need for life and godliness. I have already put it in your spirit. Now is the time to harvest the riches of My glory from the part of you that is most like Me—your spirit.

Grace is God's power to help us. It's His favor. It's His provision for us to truly live as free people. The moment I began to put this thing together on my own, His grace evaporated. I chose my own help over the help of Almighty God which, in retrospect, seems absurd. This is, of course, in hindsight, and hindsight is always 20/20.

It is actually excruciating to give up control to God. It is something He designed us to do from the beginning of time—to rely on Him and His help in every situation. But we are thousands of years downstream from the fall and everything that fell with it. The world system we were born into pushes hard against this understanding, and this system includes the church. Our soul's way, not the way of the Spirit, is the church we are used to. Be sure I am not proposing disorder; no, I am suggesting a new order that will find our churches filled with people who have made a choice to do something they've never done before. What is that choice? It's to nurture their spirit so they can truly sit in heavenly places with their brother, Jesus, and their Father, God, here in the earth. This is kingdom life; this is redeeming life. It is what Jesus stood for and demonstrated when He walked in the earth. He is passionate about our opening ourselves up to receiving ministry to our spirit. He wants our spirit to walk in partnership with the

Holy Spirit in the dominion and authority of the kingdom of God—right here and right now. Some have called this the glory dimension. It is the place of trust in God, trust He will give us the fish we ask for and not a stone.

Again, listen with your spirit to the Word of God for you:

God wants us to live as free spirits, animated and motivated by God's Spirit. Then we won't feed the compulsions of selfishness. For there is a root of sinful self-interest in us that is at odds with a free spirit, just as the free spirit is incompatible with selfishness. These two ways of life are exact opposites, so you cannot live at times one way and at times another way according to how you feel. Why don't you choose to be led by the Spirit and so escape the erratic compulsions of a law-dominated existence?

It's obvious what kind of life develops out of trying to get your own way all the time: repetitive, loveless cheap sex; a stinking accumulation of mental and emotional garbage; frenzied and joyless grabs for happiness; trinket gods; magic-show religion; paranoid loneliness; cutthroat competition; all-consuming, yet never satisfied wants; a brutal temper; an impotence to love or be loved; divided homes and divided lives; small-minded and lopsided pursuits; the vicious habit of depersonalizing everyone into a rival; uncontrolled and uncontrollable addictions; poor imitations of community. I could go on" (Galatians 5: 16-21 MSG, paraphrased).

How can we live God's way? Without a developed spirit, it is difficult if not impossible. Deliverance may come; healing may happen; but the traction we need to continue to walk in the authority of the kingdom and be true ambassadors (in this way of righteousness, peace, and joy in the Spirit) will not hold.

Just recently I received a strong lesson from the Lord. As I typed this out, I misspelled the word "lesson." I spelled it "lesion" ... which may be more accurate. I knew I had a lesion in my spirit. As I held back from God's healing hand, resisting His desire to heal me of a recurring fear, I saw a vision of my tearing His flesh, just as if I had done it myself at His crucifixion. I kept getting an image of an instrument of torture tearing the flesh of His back over and over. I knew this was the Spirit's way of showing me the hurt and pain of the Lord, Who had already paid an exorbitant price for my sin. It was very vivid. What I came to understand in my spirit was that every time I agreed with the enemy and allowed fear in, it was tearing at my Lord once again. The enemy, of course, loves this. It is a design of his, a design of hell to keep me trapped in a cell of deception and fear. I rejected this. I cried out to the Lord and said no to the enemy and his design. I took authority, resisted passivity, and pronounced I was safe and sound in my Father's care, and He alone was my protector and provider forever. He has seated me in high heaven alongside my brother and friend, Jesus, and with Him, my Father. I have the power. I have the authority!

The church has taught us to wait for a minister to lay hands on us, for someone to impart something to us, for someone to pray for us, but *we* have the authority. The same spirit that raised Jesus from the dead lives in me! Do you really believe you can capture this truth with your soul? Are you kidding? If I would speak of my own soul, I must say no; I cannot reach this truth and fulfill it in my life. In my soul I have a lot of good things, but not the divine connection with my Maker that exists in the deepest part of who I am—in my spirit.

When my soul was in control of my life, leading my spirit instead of the other way around, my soul made some decisions the world applauded and called good. I went along with that judgment at the time. Years later, I look back and see nothing but waste, vanity, confusion, and even death. God's Word says, "There is a way that appears to be right, but in the end it leads to death" (Proverbs 16:25). But praise God! Even before I had a personal relationship with Jesus Christ, my spirit connected with God. By His grace He gave my spirit the strength to choose life. His grace empowered me to get out and get help.

Now you may be saying to yourself, *That's nice, but so what?* God never intended for us to get this with just our souls. He knows how He made us and He has shown us that His design, the design of heaven, is for our spirit to rule over our soul. Look once more at I Thessalonians 5:23-24 and you will see it there: "May God himself, the God of peace, sanctify you through and through. May your whole spirit, soul and body be kept blameless at the coming of our Lord Jesus Christ. The One who calls you is faithful and he will do it." So be it. (Amen)

He *will* do it.

So be it. (Amen)

The Redemptive Gift Questionnaire

TO KNOW your position in Christ, you must first know your spiritual identity—your redemptive gift. Knowing it helps you understand who you are and who God made you to be. This will then position you to partner with God in His purposes in the earth.

The purpose of this inventory is to help you identify your redemptive gift. Each person has some measure of all seven of these gifts, because we are all made in the image of God; however, there is usually one particular heart motivation we recognize as our own—our primary redemptive gift.

As you read the questions, answer them based on your first hunch. Don't labor over your answers. There are no right or wrong answers.

PUT A "1" before the statement if it's NEVER true for you.
PUT A "2" before the statement if it's SOMETIMES true for you.
PUT A "4" before the statement if it's MOSTLY true for you.
PUT A "5" before the statement if it's ALWAYS true for you.

Your Redemptive Gift Questionnaire

1) _____ You make sure to tell the truth with accuracy.

2) _____ You keep the younger generation in mind with the things you do (children and grandchildren).

3) _____ You get very excited about organizing and putting things together.

4) _____ You can disagree with others about important things without getting your feelings hurt.

5) _____ You have a tremendous capacity to show love.

6) _____ You are quick to see what is right in a situation (and you are right about what's right).

7) _____ You can see people's practical needs and you are quick to meet them.

8) _____ You prove the truth of things by weighing it against the facts.

9) _____ You can go along with people who have different ways of looking at things.

10) _____ You are most comfortable being in authority when you are under authority yourself.

11) _____ You avoid being alone.

12) _____ You can sense the emotional atmosphere of people and places.

13) ____ You see things as either black or white.

14) ____ You enjoy showing hospitality.

15) ____ You love to study and do research.

16) ____ You will put off making a decision so that you can keep your options open as long as possible.

17) ____ You don't give up doing a job---even when you are criticized—until the job is done.

18) ____ You have no problem relating to people of different backgrounds, races, religions, or cultures, etc.

19) ____ You don't want to be in conflict with people or confront them when something's wrong.

20) ____ You can size up another person's character pretty quickly.

21) ____ You stick with anything you commit to until it's done.

22) ____ You are very serious about people using words and facts that are correct when they speak.

23) ____ You handle every situation as unique.

24) ____ You are good at managing your time.

25) ____ You love to encourage others to live victoriously.

26) ____ You feel drawn to people who are hurting or in distress.

27)____ You live your life according to principles---according to the laws of truth.

28)____ You find it hard to say no when people ask you for help.

29)____ You like to solve problems by starting out with a plan.

30)____ You look at life through the lens of relationships; that's how life makes sense to you.

31)____ You are great at motivating people to get jobs done.

32)____ You like people to show you they're interested when you speak or teach.

33)____ You have no problem recognizing a con man or someone with insincere motives.

34)__ You want to know what your own blind spots are, and you want to help others find theirs too.

35)____ You need to be appreciated.

36)____ You tend to borrow things without returning them promptly.

37)____ Family is important to you.

38)____ You are ready to move on to the next new thing once a job is done.

39)____ You are greatly loved because of your positive outlook on life.

40)____ You are careful how you speak/act so as to not hurt other people.

41)____ You have a need to tell/show others what you see around you.

42)____ You feel your greatest joy when you are doing something helpful.

43)____ You have strong opinions and convictions based upon your investigations of the facts.

44)____ You are concerned about the greater community you live in.

45)____ You thrive under pressure.

46)____ You see trials as opportunities for growth.

47)____ You let your heart rule you, not your head.

48)____ You have strong opinions and convictions.

49)____ You don't like being a leader.

50)____ You really like to write.

51)____ You see money as security.

52)____ You want to see things done as quickly as possible.

53)____ You talk with people easily.

54)____ You can sense things but are not usually able to explain how or why.

55)____ You say it like it is; you don't beat around the bush!

56)____ You want to do all you can to support those in leadership.

To Score the Questionnaire

Use the table below to organize your answers. Write the score you gave each question beside the question's number and then add up each column to get the total number for that gift. Your two highest numbers will indicate your PRIMARY and SECONDARY redemptive gifts.

1_____ 2 _____ 3 _____ 4 _____ 5 ____ 6 ____ 7 __

8_____ 9 _____ 10 _____ 11 _____ 12 _____ 13 _____ 14 __

15____ 16 _____ 17 _____ 18 _____ 19 _____ 20 _____ 21 __

22 ____ 23 _____ 24 _____ 25 _____ 26 _____ 27 _____ 28 __

29 ____ 30 _____ 31 _____ 32 _____ 33 _____ 34 _____ 35 __

36 ____ 37 _____ 38 _____ 39 _____ 40 _____ 41 _____ 42 __

43 ____ 44 _____ 45 _____ 46 _____ 47 _____ 48 _____ 49 __

50 ____ 51 _____ 52 _____ 53 _____ 54 _____ 55 _____ 56 __

TOTALS

_____   _____   _____   _____   _____   _____   __

TEACHER   GIVER   RULER   EXHORTER   MERCY   PROPHET SERVANT

MY PRIMARY REDEMPTIVE GIFT: _____

MY SECONDARY REDEMPTIVE GIFT: _____

Recommended Reading

Blessing Your Spirit by Sylvia Gunter and Arthur Burk
A series of fatherly blessings designed to grow your spirit.
Legitimacy and identity are explored.

Designed for Fulfillment by Chuck Wale
Through the transformational truths in this book, you will
understand your God-given design and be set free to accomplish
God's plan for you.

Healing the Human Spirit by Ruth Hawkeye
Describes the functions and wounding of the human spirit and
how to receive healing for this most vital part of your being.

The Inner Voice of Love by Henri Nouwen
The spiritual freedom gained from a painful journey through
anguish to freedom, as described in the author's secret journal.

Jesus Calling by Sarah Young
Daily devotions that develop the spiritual discipline of listening
to God and increasing spiritual intimacy with Him.

Business Unlimited by J. Gunnar Olson

The story of one man's obedient trust in the Holy Spirit and his conviction that faith working through love is the way to advance of the kingdom of God.

If I Perish, I Perish by Ian Thomas

A marvelous examination of the Christian life, looking specifically at the human spirit, soul, and body and their roles in relation to the Spirit of God—as told through the book of Esther.

There Were Two Trees in the Garden by Rick Joyner

We must learn to relate to Jesus spirit to Spirit, and to discern that there is truth that kills and there is the Truth (Jesus Christ) Who gives life. True spiritual vision comes when we recognize Jesus is no longer a man, but was and is fully Spirit.

I Give You Authority by Charles Kraft

Spiritual authority and power unpacked as we accept redemption—through the blood of Christ—that enables us to have relationship with God and victory over Satan.

The Power of Proclamation by Derek Prince

The tremendous power that is released through proclaiming the Word of God, which has relevance in all situations—from personal needs to international crises.

The Call by Rick Joyner

Through a series of spiritual experiences, the Lord shows the author how the church today is headed for terrible catastrophe if some very basic course corrections are not made.

My Utmost for His Highest by Oswald Chambers

A source of daily spiritual nurture, this book's strength lies in its stubborn insistence on redemption as our only secure foundation.

The Believer's Guide to Spiritual Warfare by Tom White

An insightful manual on how to stand firm, guarded, and victorious in the fight of faith by availing of your deep-rooted authority and the approval of heaven.

Pure Joy by Arthur Burk and Crystal Wade (the "pink book")

A book of blessing and instruction, the focus of which is to help parents build joy into their baby's spirit.

How to Hear God's Voice by Mark Virkler

This book shows you how to develop the ability to hear the voice of God, which is a foundational value for nurturing the inner being or spirit of man.

The Bait of Satan by John Bevere

Our spirits are made to give and receive life, but offense puts us in a stranglehold. Spiritual growth comes when we choose to humble ourselves, forgive as needed, and reconcile when possible with others.

Boundaries by Henry Cloud and John Townsend

The goal of this book is to help you use biblical boundaries appropriately to achieve the relationships and purposes God intends for you as His child.

About the Author

Dorinda Trick

DORINDA TRICK is a retired professional counselor, ordained minister, and teacher with a passion for bringing others into their true identity and legitimacy in God. Dorinda lives with her husband, Fred, and two dogs, Max and Maggie, on a beautiful bluff overlooking a river in Alabama.

Made in the USA
Charleston, SC
19 September 2015